LEAD, KINDLY LIGHT

MINUTE MEDITATIONS FOR EVERY DAY
TAKEN FROM THE WORKS
OF CARDINAL NEWMAN

Compiled and Edited
by Rev. James C. Sharp

Illustrated

CATHOLIC BOOK PUBLISHING CORP.
New Jersey

CONTENTS

NIHIL OBSTAT: James T. O'Connor, S.T.D.
Censor Librorum

IMPRIMATUR: ✠ Patrick J. Sheridan, D.D.
Vicar General, Archdiocese of New York

The Nihil Obstat and Imprimatur are official declarations that a book or a pamphlet is free of doctrinal or moral error. No implications is contained therein that those who have granted the Nihil Obstat and Imprimatur agree with the contents, opinions or statements expressed.

(T-184)

ISBN 978-0-89942-184-1

© 1993 Catholic Book Publishing Corp., N.J.
Printed in China   21 HA 2
catholicbookplishing.com

INTRODUCTION

BEFORE he passed to the Lord on the feast of All Saints, 1991, Father James Sharp put together much of this book of reflections from the great nineteenth-century writer and convert to Catholicism, John Henry Newman (1801-1890). Most of the selections are from Newman's classic work *Parochial and Plain Sermons*, written during his early years, but they reveal the fire in the soul of this great witness to the Faith.

After a number of years of inner searching and conflict as an Anglican, Newman entered the Catholic Church in 1845. Ordained in Rome in 1846, he returned to England where he began the Oratory of St. Philip Neri in Birmingham.

In 1853, Newman founded the Catholic University in Dublin and wrote his classic *The Idea of a University*. He spent much of his Catholic life in pastoral work, teaching, and writing. In 1879, he was made a Cardinal.

Newman wrote in flawless English prose. He translated the ancient Christian Faith into the language of the English-speaking world. He was a scholar, a writer, a philosopher, and a holy man.

Father Sharp has contributed to making the mind and heart of John Henry Newman better known in our world. May his words and wisdom find fertile soil in the hearts of many.

Msgr. Richard M. Liddy
Seton Hall University

PUBLISHER'S NOTE

A FEW years ago, Father Sharp approached us with the idea of putting together a book of quotations from Cardinal Newman for one of our series of meditation books. We encouraged him to prepare a manuscript.

Along the way, Father Sharp was called to his eternal reward, leaving an unfinished and unedited manuscript. However, his approach was such that our editors were able to complete his work along the lines he had started.

This book is not intended primarily as a collection of quotations from the writings of Cardinal Newman with full references for scholarly study. It is part of our "Minute Meditations Series," whose main purpose is to provide brief spiritual reading and reflection for each day.

Hence, to carry out this purpose, it has been necessary to condense and adapt Cardinal Newman's thought. For example, archaisms have been eliminated; sentences, clauses, or phrases have been deleted without indication; and gaps have been bridged by supplying words.

Through it all, we believe we have been able to achieve what Father Sharp started out to do—to retain the flavor and style of Newman for modern readers.

The prayer at the end of each reflection enables readers to apply the saintly Cardinal's ideas to their daily lives in such a way as to aid their spiritual growth.

JANUARY 1
Our Precious Faith

FOR all of us, high and low, in our measure are responsible for the safekeeping of the Faith. This Faith is what even the humblest member of the Church must contend for; and in proportion to his education, will the circle of his knowledge enlarge.

Blessed be God! We have not to find the Truth, it is put into our hands. We have but to commit it to our hearts, to preserve it inviolate, and to deliver it over to posterity. —*The Gospel a Trust*

PRAYER. Help me, O God, to believe all that You have revealed and teach through Your Holy, Catholic, and Apostolic Church.

JANUARY 2
Our Neglect of God

LET each of us reflect upon his own most gross and persevering neglect of God at various seasons of his past life. How considerate He has been to us! Yet how did we refuse to come to Him that we might have life! How did we sin against light.

He shed His Holy Spirit upon us that we might love Him. And "this is the love of God, that we keep His Commandments, and His Commandments are not grievous" (1 Jn 5:3). Why, then, have they been grievous to us?

—*God's Commandments not Grievous*

PRAYER. O God, You ever call us back to Your service. Help me to keep Your Commandments.

JANUARY 3
Appreciation of the Blessed Sacrament

GOD grant that we may be able ever to come to the Blessed Sacrament with suitable feelings. Let us not be of those who come without reverence, without awe, without wonder, without love.

But let us come in faith and hope. Let us say, "May this be the beginning to us of everlasting bliss!" May these be the firstfruits of that banquet which is to last for ever.   —*The Gospel Feast*

PRAYER. *Loving Savior, inflame my heart with love so that I may always receive Holy Communion with gratitude.*

JANUARY 4
God's Influence on Us

LET no one think it strange to say that God may be holding communion with us without our knowing it. We commonly speak of being influenced by God's grace. This implies a certain communication between the soul and God.

Yet who will say that he himself can tell when God moves him and when he is responding? God may manifest Himself to us, and that to the increase of our comfort, and yet we not realize that He does so.

—*Gospel Sign Addressed to Faith*

PRAYER. *Accept every thought, word, and deed that I perform today, O God, in union with the Sacrifice of the Mass throughout the world.*

JANUARY 5
Abraham's Call

THE commanded sacrifice of Abraham's beloved son foreshadowed the true Lamb Which God had provided for a burnt offering.

In the call of the Patriarch, in whose Seed all nations of the earth should be blessed, the great outlines of the Gospel were anticipated; in that he was called in uncircumcision, that he was justified by faith, that he trusted in God's power to raise the dead, that he looked forward to the day of Christ. —*Glory of the Christian Church*

PRAYER. *Grant me, O merciful Lord, the faith that inspired Abraham to be willing to make whatever sacrifices are necessary to please You.*

JANUARY 6
Christ Manifesting His Glory

EPIPHANY is a season set apart for adoring the glory of Christ. It leads us to the contemplation of Him as a King upon His throne.

At Christmas we commemorate His grace; in Lent His sufferings and death; on Easter Day His victory. And in all of these seasons He does something, or suffers something. But in the Epiphany we celebrate Him as an august and glorious King. —*Season of Epiphany*

PRAYER. *During the season of Epiphany, O Jesus, help me to make You known to the people of my day.*

JANUARY 7
God's Nearness to Us

ET us not seek then for signs and wonders, or ask for sensible inward tokens of God's favor. Faith only can introduce us to the unseen Presence of God. Let us venture to believe.

Almighty God is hidden from us. The utmost we can do in the way of nature is to feel after Him, Who, though we see Him not, yet is not far from every one of us.

—The Gospel Sign Addressed to Faith

PRAYER. *Not a bird falls from a tree that You, O God, do not know about. Be ever present to me so that I may rejoice in Your consolation.*

JANUARY 8
God's Adopted Children

T. John and St. Paul both teach the privilege of Christians as God's adopted children and make the grant of this and all other privileges depend on faith.

We are thus permitted more clearly to ascertain the main outlines of the Christian *character.* Love is its essence; its chief characteristics: resignation and composure of mind, neither anxious for the morrow, nor hoping from this world; and its duties: almsgiving, self-denial, prayer, and praise. *—The Gospel Witnesses*

PRAYER. *Born again through water and the Holy Spirit, may I always hope in Your promise of eternal life, dear God.*

JANUARY 9
Our Attitude toward This Life

IT is plain how we should regard this life. We should remember that we are immortal spirits and that this life is but a sort of outward stage on which we act for a time.

Our present state is precious as revealing to us the existence and attributes of Almighty God and His elect people. It is precious, because it enables us to hold communion with immortal souls who are on their trial as we are. It is momentous, as being the scene and means of our trial, but beyond this, it has no claims upon us.

—*Greatness of Human Life*

PRAYER. *Dear God, let me always realize that I am here for a time to love and serve You until You call me to eternal life.*

JANUARY 10
Prospect of Future Immortality

WHEN we take into account the powers with which our souls are gifted as Christians, the very consciousness of these fills us with a certainty that they must last beyond this life.

The greatness of these gifts, contrasted with the scanty time for exercising them, forces the mind forward to the thought of another life, as almost the necessary counterpart and consequence of this life.   —*Greatness of Human Life*

PRAYER. *O Lord, help me to realize that my destiny is to be joined to You forever in eternity.*

JANUARY 11
The Second Coming

THIS visible creation will fade away. The Sun of Righteousness, with healing on His wings, will come forth in visible form. The stars will be replaced by Saints and Angels circling His throne.

These are thoughts to make us eagerly and devoutly say, "Come, Lord Jesus, to end the time of waiting, of darkness, of turbulence, of disputing, of sorrow, of care."
—*Greatness of Human Life*

PRAYER. *Lord Jesus, when You return in glory let me hear You say, "Come, you blessed of My Father."*

JANUARY 12
Peace of a Good Conscience

IT is a difficult and rare virtue to mean what we say, to love without dissimulation, to think no evil, to bear no grudge, to be free from selfishness, to be innocent and straightforward. This character of mind is one of the surest marks of Christ's elect.

They take everything in good part which happens to them and make the best of every one. Such persons are cheerful and contented. They desire but little and take pleasure in the least matters, having no wish for riches and distinction.
—*Guilelessness*

PRAYER. *Jesus, I accept everything that comes to me in this life, both the joys and the sorrows. Help me to reflect Your Presence in my soul.*

JANUARY 13
Virtues of a Christian Life

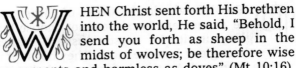

WHEN Christ sent forth His brethren into the world, He said, "Behold, I send you forth as sheep in the midst of wolves; be therefore wise as serpents and harmless as doves" (Mt 10:16).

Innocence must be joined to prudence, discretion, self-command, gravity, patience, perseverance in well-doing, but innocence is the beginning.
—Guilelessness

PRAYER. *Help me, O Lord, to practice the virtues. Do not let me become discouraged by disappointments, but let me use them to my merit.*

JANUARY 14
Our Place in God's Kingdom

OUR Lord solemnly declares that the high places of His Kingdom are not His to give. Who then are the heirs for whom the Kingdom is prepared?

He tells us expressly: those who fed the hungry and thirsty, lodged the stranger, clothed the naked, visited the sick, came to the prisoners, for His sake. To whom is it that He will say, "Enter into the joy of your Lord"?—to those whom He can praise as "good and faithful servants" (Mt 25:21).
—Human Responsibility

PRAYER. *May I, O Lord, hear You tell me to take my place with Your Angels and Saints in heaven.*

JANUARY 15
The Glory of the Cross

PERSONS who in the Cross of Christ see the Atonement for sin cannot choose but glory in it. Its mysteriousness makes them glory in it the more. They boast of it before men and Angels, before an unbelieving world, and before fallen spirits.

They confess this miracle of grace and cherish it in their creed, though it gains them but contempt.   *—Humiliation of the Eternal Son*

PRAYER. *Praised be Jesus Christ Who has redeemed the world by His Life, Death, and Resurrection!*

JANUARY 16
Basic Christian Truths

MAY God the Father give us a heart and understanding to realize, as well as to confess, that doctrine into which we were baptized.

His Only-begotten Son, our Lord, was conceived by the Holy Spirit, was born of the Virgin Mary, suffered, and was buried, rose again from the dead, ascended into heaven, whence He shall come again, at the end of the world, to judge the living and the dead.

—Humiliation of the Eternal Son

PRAYER. *Dear God, let the recitation of the Creed at Mass remind me of the marvels that You have revealed about Your life and the things that have been done for my salvation.*

JANUARY 17
Seeing Christ's Future Glory

THE time will come, if we be found worthy, when we, who now see in a glass darkly, shall see our Lord and Savior face to face. We shall behold His countenance beaming with the fullness of Divine Perfections, and bearing its own witness that He is the Son of God.

Let us then praise and bless Him in the Church. —*The Incarnation*

PRAYER. *May the pouring out of Your Holy Spirit, Lord, be cause for my seeing You in Your heavenly Kingdom.*

JANUARY 18
Eternity Our Goal

ENDEAVOR to disengage your thoughts and opinions from the things that are seen; look at things as God looks at them and judge them as He judges.

When the fever of life is over, and you are waiting in silence for the judgment, who can say how dreadful may be the memory of sins done in the body? Then the very apprehension of their punishment will doubtless outweigh a thousandfold the gratification, such as it was, which you felt in committing them.

—*Individuality of the Soul*

PRAYER. *Loving Father, I am sorry for my sins because I dread the loss of heaven and the pains of hell, but most of all, because they offend You.*

JANUARY 19
The Souls of the Dead Live On

CHRIST says: "Many are called, few are chosen"; "Broad is the way that leads to destruction, and many there be who go in that path"; whereas "Narrow is the way that leads to life" (Mt 7:13-14).

It is difficult to realize that all who ever lived still live; it is as difficult to believe that they are in a state of eternal rest or of eternal woe.

—Individuality of the Soul

PRAYER. *Blessed Jesus, through the merits of Your Passion and Death, allow me to be a sharer of Your glory in the life to come.*

JANUARY 20
Christian Regeneration

THIS wonderful change from darkness to light, through the entrance of the Spirit into the soul, is called Regeneration, or the New Birth; a blessing which is now conveyed to all men freely through Baptism.

By nature we are children of wrath; the heart is sold under sin, possessed by evil spirits, and inherits death as its eternal portion. But by the coming of the Holy Spirit, all guilt and pollution are burned away, the devil is driven forth, sin is forgiven, and the whole man is consecrated to God.

—Indwelling Spirit

PRAYER. *You have given me a new birth, O God, by water and the Holy Spirit. May I possess these gifts until my death.*

JANUARY 21
Corporate Worship

TRESS is to be laid upon the duty of united worship. "Where two or three are gathered together in His name, He is in the midst of them" (Mt 18:20).

Christ is so one with them, that they are not their own, they lose for the time their earth-strains. Viewed as one, the Church is still His image as at the first, pure and spotless, His spouse all-glorious within, the Mother of Saints.

—*Glory of the Church*

PRAYER. *Help me realize, O God, that when I join together with others in offering the Holy Sacrifice of the Mass, I am joined to countless others all over the world who praise You.*

JANUARY 22
Channels of Redemption

T is certain from Scripture that the gift of reconciliation is not conveyed to individuals except through appointed ordinances. Sacraments are the channels of the peculiar Christian privileges, and not merely *seals* of the covenant.

Though Christ has purchased inestimable blessings for our race, yet it is still necessary to apply them to individuals by visible means.

—*Christian Ministry*

PRAYER. *My Savior, You have left me the Sacraments as a means of increasing Your grace in my soul. Let me always be grateful.*

JANUARY 23
Sorrow for Sin

LET us but consider how we have fallen from the light and grace of our Baptism. We must renew our confession, and seek afresh our absolution day by day.

Whatever affliction meets us through life, we must take it as a merciful penance imposed by a Father upon erring children, to remind us of the weight of that infinitely greater punishment, which was our desert by nature, and which Christ bore for us on the Cross.—*Indwelling Spirit*

PRAYER. *Merciful God, I am sorry for my sins. Help me to never sin again.*

JANUARY 24
The Spirit of God Prompts Us

WHERE the Holy Spirit is, "there is liberty" from the tyranny of sin. Doubt, gloom, impatience have been expelled; joy in the Gospel has taken their place.

Thus the Spirit of God creates in us the simplicity and warmth of heart which children have, nay, rather the perfections of His heavenly hosts, high and low; for what are implicit trust, ardent love, abiding purity, but the mind both of little children and of the adoring Seraphim!
—*Indwelling Spirit*

PRAYER. *Send Your Holy Spirit on me, O God, and inspire me ever to be mindful of the physical and spiritual needs of others.*

JANUARY 25
The Spirit Renews Us

THE Holy Spirit dwells in body and soul as in a temple. He is able to search into all our thoughts and penetrate into every motive of the heart. Therefore He pervades us as light pervades a building.

In Scripture language we are said to be in Him, and He in us. It is plain that such an inhabitation brings the Christian into a state altogether new and marvelous and gives him a place and an office which he had not before.

—*Indwelling Spirit*

PRAYER. *Shine through me, O Jesus, and let me be a light to all with whom I come into contact.*

JANUARY 26
The Blessed Happiness of Heaven

BLESSED they who are destined for the sight of those wonders in which they now stand, at which they now look, but which they do not recognize!

They are immortal and eternal. The souls who shall then be made conscious of them will see them in their calmness and their majesty where they ever have been. Who can imagine the feelings of those who, having died in faith, wake up to enjoyment! The life then begun, we know, will last for ever.

—*Invisible World*

PRAYER. *My Lord and my God, help me to understand that when I am joined to You in eternity, all will be revealed.*

JANUARY 27
Beginning of Wisdom

I N a Christian, *fear and love must go to-gether*. In heaven, love will absorb fear; but in this world, *fear and love must go to-gether*. No one can love God aright without fearing Him, though many fear Him and yet do not love Him.

Self-confident men do not fear God and they think this bold freedom is to love Him. Deliberate sinners fear but cannot love Him. But devotion to Him consists in love and fear.

—*Christian Reverence*

PRAYER. *Merciful Lord, please bless me with the precious gifts of reverent fear and sincere love.*

JANUARY 28
Accept God's Grace

Y OU do not know what will become of you, unless you receive the gifts of grace when they are offered. Perhaps you will rush into open and willful sin. Your heart may be upon the world; you may pass through life with no love of things invisible, no love of Christ your Savior.

This will be the end of your refusing the love compulsion of Almighty God: slavery to this world, and to the god of this world. God save us all, young and old, from this, through Jesus Christ. —*Acceptance of Religious Privileges*

PRAYER. *My Lord and my God, let me always be attentive to the promptings of Your grace.*

JANUARY 29
Acting Like a Christian

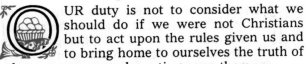 UR duty is not to consider what we should do if we were not Christians but to act upon the rules given us and to bring home to ourselves the truth of them, as we go on, by acting upon them.

Non-Christians indeed may be bound to go into the question of evidences, but our duty is to use the talents of which we find ourselves possessed, and to essay their genuineness by deeds, not by arguments. —*Acceptance of Privileges*

PRAYER. *I believe, dear Lord, all that You have revealed and Your Church teaches. Help me when I am inclined to doubt.*

JANUARY 30
Christ Has Done All for Us

AN anyone enter into the doctrine of the Atonement without possessing a clear assurance that there is nothing in the world that can be done for us which Christ has not done and will not do?

By His sighs and tears, by His agony and death, by all He has suffered, He seems to entreat us to have confidence in Him. He entreats us to take on trust the truth that we are compelled to receive God's mercies, yet punished for the misuse of them. —*Acceptance of Privileges*

PRAYER. *My Savior, there is nothing You could have done for me that You have not done. Never let me depart from my love for You.*

21

JANUARY 31
Doing Everything for God

THIS world is a very little thing to give up for the next. Let us aim at the consistent habit of mind of looking toward God and rejoicing in the glory which shall be revealed. In that case, whether we eat or drink, or abstain, or whatever we do, we shall do all for Him.

Let us aim at being true heirs of the promise. Let us aspire to be holy and undefiled, "blameless and harmless, in the midst of a perverse nation" (Phil 2:15).   —*Apostolic Abstinence*

PRAYER. *O Lord, when I perform acts of self-denial, accept them in reparation for my sins and for Your glory.*

FEBRUARY 1
Uniting Our Sufferings to Christ's

IN considering the benefits of trial and suffering, we should never forget that these things by themselves have no power to make us holier. It is only in the hands of God that we are God's instruments.

It is only when grace is in the heart, when power from above dwells in a man, that anything outward or inward turns to his salvation. God alone can work, and He can work through all things.   —*Affliction, a School of Comfort*

PRAYER. *O Jesus, let me unite my sufferings with Your Passion and Death so that they may be a means of furthering my salvation.*

FEBRUARY 2
Fellowship of the Baptized

LET us feel tenderly toward all whom Christ has made His own by Baptism. Let us sympathize with them and have kind thoughts toward them. Let us pray for their growth in faith and holiness.

"Let us not love in word but in deed and in truth" (1 Jn 3:18). For "God is love" (1 Jn 4:8). If we love one another, "God dwells in us, and His love is perfected in us" (1 Jn 4:12).

—*Communion of Saints*

PRAYER. *Assist with Your grace, O Lord, all who have been made Your followers by Baptism. May all who call on You be united in Faith.*

FEBRUARY 3
Zeal for the Things of God

THE Old Testament especially teaches us that zeal is as essentially a duty of all God's rational creatures as prayer and praise, faith and submission.

Zeal consists in a strict attention to His commands, an intense thirst for the advancement of His glory, a shrinking from the pollution of sin, and an indignation at witnessing His honor insulted. It demands a heroic determination to yield Him service at whatever sacrifice of personal feeling. —*Jewish Zeal, a Pattern to Christians*

PRAYER. *Almighty God, let zeal for the things of religion and love of my neighbor motivate me every day of my life.*

FEBRUARY 4
Our Way to Heaven

T was the untold sufferings of the Eternal Word in our nature which has put away from us the wrath of Him Whose love sent Him for that very purpose.

Thus, in a most mysterious way, all that is needful for this sinful world, the life of our souls, the regeneration of our nature flow from a fount of blood. A work of blood is our salvation. We must draw near in faith and accept it as the way to heaven. —*Bodily Suffering*

PRAYER. *O Lord, by Your Passion and Death, You have made us children of God. Let me keep Your Commandments so that I may one day share Your glory.*

FEBRUARY 5
Catholic Church Our Guide

E have need to watch against narrowness of mind lest we suppose ourselves to have such a clear knowledge of God's ways, as to rely implicitly on our own notions.

In this perplexity of mind the Church Catholic is our divinely intended guide. She keeps us from a narrow interpretation of Scripture, from local prejudices, and excitements of the day. —*Contracted Views in Religion*

PRAYER. *In Your mercy, O Lord, You have instituted the Church to be the guide of Your people. Help me to put her teachings into practice.*

FEBRUARY 6
Reverence and Faith

SO natural is the connection between a reverential spirit in worshiping God and faith in God that the wonder only is how anyone can for a moment imagine he has faith in God and yet allow himself to be irreverent toward Him.

To believe in God is to believe the being and presence of One Who is All-holy, and All-powerful, and All-gracious; how can a man really believe thus of Him and yet make free with Him? —*Reverence in Worship*

PRAYER. *Let my faith in You, O my God, lead me to serve You with a reverential love.*

FEBRUARY 7
Privilege of Praising God

ALL holy creatures are praising God continually—we hear them not, still they are praising Him. All the Angels, the glorious company of the Apostles, the Holy Church universal, all the spirits and souls of the righteous, all are praising and praying to God.

We come to church to join them. We do not deserve to come—consider what a great favor it is to be allowed to join in the praises and prayers of the City of God. —*Reverence in Worship*

PRAYER. *O Eternal Beauty, may my greatest joy be to praise You all my days here on earth and forever in heaven.*

FEBRUARY 8
God, a Gentle Task-master

LET us beg of God the spirit of faith and hope that we may not account Him a hard master. Let us learn lovingly to adore the hand that afflicts us and to kiss the rod, however sharply or long it smites us.

Let us look on to the end of all things and to the coming of Christ which will at length save us and not faint on the rough way, nor toss upon our couch of thorns. —*Chastisement amid Mercy*

PRAYER. *Dear Lord, help me to understand that whatever happens to me in this life can be a means of merit for me toward eternity. Give me the grace to persevere in Your service.*

FEBRUARY 9
Surrendering Ourselves to God

WE are all more or less sinners against God's grace, many of us grievous sinners. God may spare us, He may punish. In either case, however, our duty is to surrender ourselves into His hands that He may do what He will.

Let us beg of Him not to forsake us in our miserable state. Let us ask Him to enable us to hate sin truly and confess it honestly and to bear His judgments cheerfully.

—*Chastisement amid Mercy*

PRAYER. *Your mercy, O Lord, endures forever. Look upon me in Your love and let me always surrender myself to You.*

FEBRUARY 10
Hear His Voice

CHRIST calls us now. There is nothing extraordinary in His dealings with us. He works through our natural faculties and circumstances of life.

Still what happens to us in providence is in all essential respects what His voice was to those whom He addressed when on earth: whether He commands by a visible presence, or by a voice, or by our consciences, it matters not, so that we feel it to be a command.—*Divine Calls*

PRAYER. *Loving Father, You said, "This is My beloved Son, listen to Him." May I hear His voice whenever He calls.*

FEBRUARY 11
The Sacrament of Our Salvation

BEFORE He went away, Jesus completed His work, bequeathing to us a special mode of approaching Him, a Holy Mystery, in which we receive that Heavenly Body, which is the life of all that believe. This is the Blessed Sacrament.

Feasting upon the Sacrifice, we may be "partakers of the Divine Nature" and the "exceeding great promises" (2 Pt 1:4) which are made to those who partake of it. —*Christ, a Quickening Spirit*

PRAYER. *Ever-loving Jesus, You have given Your Church Your Body and Blood as nourishment for our souls. Do not let me ever take this great gift for granted.*

FEBRUARY 12
Christ the New Adam

A S Adam is the author of death to the whole race, so is Christ the Origin of immortality. When Adam ate the forbidden fruit, it was as a poison spreading through his whole nature, thus through every one of his descendants.

Adam spreads poison. Christ diffuses life eternal. Christ communicates life to us by that holy and incorrupt nature which He assumed for our redemption. —*Christ, a Quickening Spirit*

PRAYER. *Blessed Savior, You restored to the human race what was lost through the sin of Adam. Make me worthy of eternal life with You.*

FEBRUARY 13
Christ's Followers Will Triumph

N OTHING can harm those who bear Christ within them. Trial or temptation, time of tribulation, time of wealth, nothing can "separate us from the love of God, which is in Christ Jesus" (Rom 8:39).

We, in this age of the world, over and above the Apostle's word, have the experience of many centuries for our comfort. We have his own history to show us how Christ within us is stronger than the world around us and will prevail. —*Christ, a Quickening Spirit*

PRAYER. *May Christ ever triumph over the forces of evil. May He give to His followers the consolation that with Him, they too will triumph.*

FEBRUARY 14
Christ's Immortality

WHEN the Word of Life was manifested in our flesh, the Holy Spirit displayed that creative hand by which, in the beginning, Eve was formed; and the Holy Child, thus conceived by the power of the Highest, was immortal even in His mortal nature, sinless and incorruptible.

Death "had no dominion over Him" (Rom 6:19). He was in the words of the text, "the Living among the dead" (Lk 24:5).

—*Christ, a Quickening Spirit*

PRAYER. *Christ's rising from the dead, O God, has filled the hearts of His followers with joy. Let me be joined in glory to the Saints.*

FEBRUARY 15
Christ's Saving Grace

SUCH is our risen Savior in Himself and toward us: conceived by the Holy Spirit; dying, but abhorring corruption; rising again by His own inherent life; exalted as the Son of God and Son of Man, to raise us after Him; and filling us incomprehensibly with His immortal nature. How wonderful a work of grace!

Strange it was that Adam should be our death but stranger still that God Himself should be our life!

—*Christ, a Quickening Spirit*

PRAYER. *Jesus, my Savior, You suffered, died, and rose again for my sake. Keep me close to You, every day of my life.*

FEBRUARY 16
Frequent Communion and Holiness

BLESSED are they if they knew their blessedness who are allowed, as we are, week after week, to seek and find the Savior of their souls! Blessed are they who are allowed to eat and drink the Food of immortality and receive life from the bleeding side of the Son of God!

Alas! By what strange coldness of heart or perverse superstition is it that anyone called Christian keeps away from that heavenly banquet?

—*Christ, a Quickening Spirit*

PRAYER. *Blessed Savior, You have given me the privilege of receiving You in Holy Communion. Help me to appreciate this marvelous gift.*

FEBRUARY 17
Lent—a Time of Great Grace

WE are now approaching the season when we commemorate Christ's death upon the Cross. We are entering upon the most holy season of the whole year. May we renew our resolutions of leading a life of obedience to His Commandments and may we have the grace to seal our good resolutions at His most sacred Supper.

It is useless to make resolves without coming to Him for aid to keep them. —*Moses, Type of Christ*

PRAYER. *May this Lent, O Lord, be an opportunity for me to be renewed spiritually. Assist me to carry out my Lenten resolutions.*

FEBRUARY 18
Quiet Perseverance

MEANTIME, while Satan only threatens, let us possess our hearts in patience; try to keep quiet; aim at obeying God in all things, little as well as great; do the duties of our calling which lie before us, day by day.

"Take no thought for the morrow, for sufficient unto the day is the evil thereof" (Mt 6:34).
—*Christ, a Quickening Spirit*

PRAYER. Blessed Lord, in the midst of the turmoil of the world and the bad example of prominent people, let me always be firm in my commitment to You.

FEBRUARY 19
God's Secret Servants

CHRIST, the sinless Son of God, might be living now in the world as our next-door neighbor and perhaps we not find it out. This should be dwelt on.

Such neighbors make no great show, they go on in the same quiet ordinary way as others but really they are training to be Saints in heaven. They do all they can to change themselves, to obey God. But they do it in secret, both because God tells them so to do and because they do not like it to be known.
—*Christ Hidden*

PRAYER. Dear Savior, do not let me be misled by judging others whose hidden lives are pleasing to You. Help me to see You in others.

FEBRUARY 20
Christ's Hidden Presence

WHEN Jesus was born into the world, the world knew it not. Now He is present upon a table. And faith adores, but the world passes by.

Let us then pray Him ever to enlighten our understanding that we may belong to the Heavenly Host, not to this world. As the carnal-minded would not perceive Him even in heaven, so the spiritual heart may approach Him, see Him, even upon earth. —*Christ Hidden*

PRAYER. *Blessed Savior, present in the Sacrament of Your love, help me to appreciate that You are always near to me when I call on You.*

FEBRUARY 21
Lent Prepares Us for Easter

THOUGH the long season of Lent which ushers in the Blessed Day of Easter in a sense quells the keenness of our enjoyment, yet without such preparatory season, we shall not rejoice at all.

None rejoice in Eastertide less than those who have not grieved in Lent. Feast day and fast day, holy tide and other tide, are one and the same to them. They do not realize the next world at all. —*Keeping Fast*

PRAYER. *During Lent, O Lord, I must make an effort to establish my own course of conduct of prayer and mortification. Help me to live up to my resolutions.*

FEBRUARY 22
Meditating on Christ's Sufferings

DEEP feeling is but the natural or necessary attendant on a holy heart. But though we cannot at our will thus feel, we can grow in grace till we do.

We may meditate upon Christ's sufferings. By this meditation we *shall* gradually be brought to these deep feelings. We may pray God to do for us what we cannot do for ourselves, to *make* us feel; to give us the spirit of gratitude, repentance, and lively faith. —*Christ's Privations*

PRAYER. *Help me, O Lord, to appreciate what You have done for me by the sufferings You endured for my sake.*

FEBRUARY 23
Jesus Christ Is Truly God

IN the Gospel, Jesus says, "Before Abraham was, I am" (Jn 8:58). He declares that He did not begin to exist from the Virgin's womb but had been in existence before. By using the words, *I am,* He seems to allude to the Name of God revealed to Moses in the burning bush when he was commanded to say to the children of Israel, "*I am* has sent me to you" (Ex 3:14).

St. John says, "In the beginning was the Word, and the Word was with God, and the Word was God" (Jn 1:1). —*Son of God Made Man*

PRAYER. *Dear Jesus, You emptied Yourself of the glory that was Yours from all eternity. Help me always to be profoundly grateful.*

FEBRUARY 24
Christ Will See You Through

DOUBT not Christ's power to bring you through any difficulties. He has showed you the way. He gave up the home of His mother Mary to "be about His Father's business" (Lk 2:49). Now He but bids you take up after Him the Cross which He bore for you.

Be not afraid. He is most gracious and will bring you on by little and little.—*Christian Manhood*

PRAYER. Through the merits of Christ my Savior, O God, help me to meet the responsibilities that my Faith imposes on me.

FEBRUARY 25
Promise of the Spirit

WHEN our Lord was leaving His Apostles, He consoled them by the promise of another Guide and Teacher—the Third Person in the Ever-blessed Trinity, the Spirit of Himself and of His Father, Who should come with great power and comfort.

The special way in which God the Holy Spirit gave glory to God the Son seems to have been His revealing Him as the Only-begotten Son of the Father, Who had appeared as the Son of Man. —*Christ Manifested*

PRAYER. God my Father, You sent Your Spirit on the Church to strengthen, enlighten, and guide her. Let me also partake of His gifts.

FEBRUARY 26
Gratitude to the Savior

THE Son of God came down from heaven, put aside His glory, and submitted to be despised, cruelly treated, and put to death by His own creatures—by those whom He had made and whom He had preserved.

Is it reasonable that so great an event should not move us? Does it not stand to reason that we must be in a very irreligious state of mind unless we have some little love, some little awe, some little repentance, in consequence of what He has done and suffered for us?   —*Christ's Privations*

PRAYER. *Jesus my Savior, I am ashamed that I have returned so little of Your love. Give me the strength to make amends.*

FEBRUARY 27
Our Future in God's Hands

GOD does not show you where He is leading you; you might be frightened if you see the whole prospect at once. I can well believe that you have hopes now, which you cannot give up. Whether they will be fulfilled, or not, is in His hand. He may be pleased to grant the desires of your heart. If so, thank Him for His mercy; only be sure that all will be for your highest good.

—*Christian Manhood*

PRAYER. *Help me, O Lord, to rely on Your grace to meet the unknown future.*

FEBRUARY 28
Maturing in Christ

HEN we outgrow our childhood, we but approach God's likeness, Who has no youth nor age, and Who is supremely blessed, because He is supremely holy.

Let us beware of indulging a mere barren faith and love, which dreams instead of working. For the Holy Spirit is the Author of active good works and leads us to the observance of all lowly deeds of ordinary obedience as the most pleasing sacrifice to God.—*Christian Manhood*

PRAYER. *Dearest God, assist me by Your grace to be a mature Christian. Help me to be a doer and not a dreamer.*

FEBRUARY 29
The World Is a Passing Attraction

S regards this world with all its enjoyments, let us not trust it. Let us "seek first the Kingdom of God and His righteousness" and then all those things of this world "will be added to us" (Mt 6:33).

They alone are able truly to enjoy this world who begin with the world unseen. They alone are able to use the world who have learned not to abuse it. They alone inherit it who take it as a shadow of the world to come.   —*Cross of Christ*

PRAYER. *Help me, O God, to realize that I am here on earth to know, love, and serve You. Do not let me be distracted from this goal.*

MARCH 1
Lenten Observances

LET those who attempt to make Lent profitable to their souls, by such observances as have ever been in use at this season since Christianity was, beware lest they lose this world without gaining the next, for instance, by relapsing. Or again, by observing what is in itself right in a cold and formal manner.

We can use the means, but it is God alone who blesses them. —*Apostolic Abstinence*

PRAYER. Never allow me, O Lord, to perform acts of self-denial during Lent simply out of routine or to be seen by others.

MARCH 2
Priest, Prophet, and King

CHRIST is a Prophet, as revealing the will of God and the Gospel of Grace. So also were the Apostles; "He that hears you, hears Me" (Lk 10:16).

Christ is a Priest, as forgiving sin, and imparting other needful divine gifts. The Apostles, too, had this power; "Whose sins you remit, they are remitted" (Jn 20:23). Christ is a King, as ruling the Church, and the Apostles rule it in His stead. "I appoint to you a Kingdom, as My Father has appointed to Me" (Lk 21:29). —*Christian Ministry*

PRAYER. Almighty Father, help me to be attentive to the voice of Christ my Teacher and to submit myself to His tender rule.

MARCH 3
Doubts Cannot Harm Us

LET us get rid of curious and presumptuous thoughts by going about our business. Let us mock and baffle the doubts which Satan whispers to us by acting against them.

The rest will follow in time; part in this world, part in the next. Doubts may pain, but they cannot harm, unless we give way to them. We ought not to give way, our conscience tells us, so that our course is plain.

—Christian Mysteries

PRAYER. *Grant, Almighty God, that I may resist all temptations to doubt by quickly acting against them.*

MARCH 4
Seeking God's Grace

CHRIST does not merely tell us that we cannot come to Him of ourselves, but He tells us also with Whom the power of coming is lodged, with His Father— that we may seek it of Him.

When we feel within us a longing after this world, let us pray God to draw us; and though we cannot move a step without Him, at least let us try to move.

—Christian Mysteries

PRAYER. *Loving Father, help me to seek Jesus with all my heart, to find Him, and to remain close to Him always.*

MARCH 5
Created for a Unique Purpose

I AM created to do something or to be something for which no one else is created; I have a place in God's counsels, in God's world, which no one else has; whether I be rich or poor, despised or esteemed by man, God knows me and calls me by my name.

God has created me to do Him some definite service; He has committed some work to me which He has not committed to another. I have my mission. —*Meditations*

PRAYER. *Merciful God, it is a great comfort to know that You have created each person for a unique purpose. Accomplish in me Your holy will.*

MARCH 6
Sufferers with Christ

WE must take Christ Who suffered as our guide. We must embrace His sacred feet and follow Him.

No wonder, then, should we receive on ourselves some drops of the sacred agony which bedewed His garments! No wonder should we be sprinkled with the sorrows which He bore in expiation of our sins!

—*Bodily Suffering*

PRAYER. *Blessed Lord, Jesus, You willingly laid down Your life for my redemption. Let me realize that I must also take up my cross daily and follow after You.*

MARCH 7
Lenten Acts of Self-denial

ET us put off the world and put on Christ. The receding from one is an approach to the other. We have now for weeks been trying, through His grace, to unclothe ourselves of earthly wants and desires. May that unclothing be for us a clothing of things invisible and imperishable!

May we grow in grace and in the knowledge of our Lord and Savior, season after season, year after year, till He takes us to Himself.

—*Difficulty of Realizing Privileges*

PRAYER. *Dear Lord, strengthen me to perform voluntarily little acts of self-denial so as to atone for my sins and gain Your merit.*

MARCH 8
God Calms Our Fears

E cannot understand Christ's mercies till we understand His power, His glory, His ineffable holiness, and our faults; that is, until we first fear Him. Not that fear comes first, and then love. For the most part they will proceed together.

Fear is allayed by the love of Him, and our love sobered by our fear of Him. Thus He draws us on with encouraging voice.

—*Christian Reverence*

PRAYER. *Almighty and eternal God, trusting in Your mercy I ask for the gift of true repentance.*

MARCH 9
Using the World Prudently

CONCERNING the things which the world admires, we may draw the following rule. Use them with gratitude for what is really good in them and with a desire to promote God's glory by means of them. But do not go out of the way to seek them. They will not make you happier and they may make you less religious.

For us, who are all the adopted children of God our Savior, what addition is wanting to complete our happiness? *—Temporal Advantages*

PRAYER. *Never allow, O Lord, the things of the world so to consume me that I lose sight of my eternal destiny.*

MARCH 10
Praying at Stated Times

STATED times of prayer are necessary, first as a means of making the mind sober and the general temper more religious.

Secondly, they are necessary as a means of exercising earnest faith, and thereby of receiving a more certain blessing in answer than we would otherwise obtain. *—Times of Private Prayer*

PRAYER. *O Lord, grant me an awareness of the need to pray with regularity. Let Your Spirit prompt me to carry out patterned prayer so that my prayers may be a source of holiness for me.*

MARCH 11
Manifestation of Christ's Divinity

JESUS was obedient unto death to atone for our sins. There the triumph of His enemies ended—ended with what was necessary for our redemption.

Immediately some tokens showed that the real victory was with Him—the earthquake and other wonders in heaven and earth. These were enough to justify His claim in the judgment of the centurion who said at once, "Truly this *was* the Son of God" (Mt 27:54).   —*Christ, a Quickening Spirit*

PRAYER. *Your Divine Son, O God, was obedient to death for my sake. May I always be grateful for what He has done.*

MARCH 12
God Is All-merciful

WHATEVER has been your past life, God's mercies in Christ are offered to you. Come to Him for them; approach Him and you shall find Him.

Let not your past sins keep you from Him. Whatever they be, they cannot interfere with His grace stored up for all who come to Him for it. Keeping from Him is not to escape from His power, only from His love. Surrender yourselves to Him in faith and holy fear. —*The Church*

PRAYER. *Sovereign Lord, through Christ's Redemption, my sins are forgiven. Let me always repent and seek Your mercy whenever I offend You.*

MARCH 13
Seeking the Creator

MAN seeks the creature when the world distresses him. Let us seek the Creator. Let us "seek the Lord and His strength" (Ps 105:4).

Great benefit indeed beyond thought, thus to ally ourselves with the upper creation of God instead of taking our portion with the lower! Can anything of this world impart such strength as He Who is present in that Sanctuary which He has given us?
—*The Church*

PRAYER. *Lord Jesus, let me always be mindful that I have here no abiding city. Help me to seek You in everything I do.*

MARCH 14
Turning to Christ on His Cross

AWAKE, then, with this season of Lent, to meet your Lord, Who now summons you from His Cross. Stand ready to suffer with Him that you may rise together with Him.

He can write the Law on your hearts and thereby take away the old curse which by nature you inherit. He has done this for many in times past. Why should He not do it for you?
—*Moses the Type of Christ*

PRAYER. *Make me, O Lord, understand how much Your love has done for me. I offer You my little acts of self-sacrifice in union with those of Yours on the Cross.*

MARCH 15
The Great Virtue of Charity

NO repentance is truly such without love. It is love which gives it its efficacy in God's sight. Without love there may be remorse, regret, self-reproach, but there is not saving penitence.

There may be conviction of the reason, but not conversion of the heart. A great many lament in themselves this want of love in repenting. They cannot abstain from any indulgence ever so trivial, which would be a natural way of showing sorrow. —*Love, the One Thing Needful*

PRAYER. *Charity, O Lord, is the greatest of virtues. Inspire me with this virtue so that I may truly turn from sin and repent.*

MARCH 16
Thinking Constantly about Christ

WHAT is meditating on Christ? It is simply this, thinking habitually and constantly of Him and of His deeds and sufferings.

It is to have Him before our minds as One Whom we may contemplate, worship, and address when we rise up, when we lie down, when we eat and drink, when we are at home and abroad, when we are working, or walking, or at rest, when we are alone, and again when we are in company. —*Christ's Privations*

PRAYER. *O Jesus, may You be always on my mind wherever I am or whatever I am doing.*

44

MARCH 17
Climate for Peace of Soul

ALL places possess their peculiar temptation. Quietness and peace, those greatest of blessings, constitute the trial of the Christians who enjoy them.

On the one hand, a religious man may thrive even in the world's pestilent air and on unwholesome food. So, on the other hand, he may become sickly, unless he guards against it, from the very abundance of privileges vouchsafed to him in a peaceful lot. —*Contracted Views in Religion*

PRAYER. *Heavenly Father, help me to understand that I can grow in Your love and service in every circumstance of life.*

MARCH 18
Danger of Overconfidence

THIS is how I describe the state into which the blessing of peace leads unwary Christians. They become not only overconfident of their knowledge of God's ways but positive in their overconfidence.

They find it a much more comfortable view, much more agreeable to the indolence of human nature, to give over seeking and to believe they had nothing more to find.

—*Contracted Views in Religion*

PRAYER. *O Almighty and Eternal God, do not let me be presumptuous but ever let me rely on Your promise of grace.*

MARCH 19
Remorse Due to Sin

IS not the pain of a bad conscience different from any other pain that we know? Can that pain be compensated by the wages of sin, or rather, does it not remain distinctly perceptible in the midst of them?

The pain which it inflicts on us is a sort of indication how God regards, and will one day visit, all sins, according to the sure word of Scripture.

—Law of the Spirit

PRAYER. *My conscience tells me, O Lord, when I have offended You. Let this prompting be cause for seeking Your forgiveness.*

MARCH 20
God Does Not Abandon Us

GOD works wondrously in the world and at certain eras His providence puts on a new aspect. Religion seems to be failing when it is merely changing its form. God seems for an instant to desert His own.

The Christian must take everything as God's gift, hold fast his *principles*, not give *them* up because appearances are for the moment against them, but believe all things will come round at length.

—Contracted Views in Religion

PRAYER. *Holy Spirit of God, inspire me with Your grace to understand what is going on in the world and in the Church. Let me be in tune with the Church.*

MARCH 21
Appreciating Christ's Passion

HOW little is our pain, our hardships, compared with those which Christ voluntarily undertook for us! If He, the Sinless, underwent these, what wonder is it that we sinners should endure the hundredth part of them?

If we felt them as we ought, they would be to us, at seasons such as that now coming, far worse than what the death of a friend is. We should not be able at such times to take pleasure in this world. —*Christ's Privations*

PRAYER. *Let me acknowledge that the cares of the world are little in comparison with the sufferings You have endured for me, O Jesus.*

MARCH 22
Sharing Christ's Passion

DURING Passiontide especially are we called upon to raise our hearts to Christ, to have keen feelings of sorrow and shame, of gratitude, of love and tender affection, and horror and anguish, at the review of those awful sufferings whereby our salvation has been purchased.

Let us pray God to give us the *beauty* of holiness, which consists in tender and eager affection toward our Lord and Savior. —*The Crucifixion*

PRAYER. *During this week we call holy, dear Jesus, let me be mindful of what my redemption has cost You. Grant me true sorrow for my sins.*

MARCH 23
Christ's Cross Gives Perspective

IT is the death of the Eternal Word of God made flesh which is our great lesson on how to think and how to speak of this world. His Cross has put its due value upon everything we see, upon all fortunes, all advantages, all dignities, all pleasures.

It has taught us how to live, how to use this world, what to expect, what to desire, what to hope. It is the tone into which all the strains of this world's music are ultimately to be resolved.

—*Cross of Christ*

PRAYER. *By Your Cross, O Blessed Savior, You have given Christians a new perspective on life. Let me see everything in light of the Cross.*

MARCH 24
Christ's Sacrifice—the Foundation

THE sacred doctrine of Christ's Atoning Sacrifice is the vital principle on which the Christian lives. Without it no other doctrine is held profitably.

To believe in Christ's Divinity or in His manhood or in the Holy Trinity or in a judgment to come or in the resurrection of the dead is an untrue belief, not Christian Faith, unless we receive also the doctrine of Christ's sacrifice.

—*Cross of Christ*

PRAYER. *You emptied Yourself, O Savior, and took a human nature for our salvation. Help me to realize all You have done for me.*

MARCH 25
Mary and Jesus United

AS to Mary, Christ derived His manhood from her, and so had an especial unity of nature with her; and this wondrous relationship between God and man it is perhaps impossible for us to dwell much upon.

We had better only think of her with her Son, never separating her from Him, but using her name as a memorial of His great condescension in stooping from heaven, and not abhorring the Virgin's womb. —*Reverence Due to Mary*

PRAYER. *Dear Jesus, Your Holy Mother cooperated with the divine plan for the human race. Let me try to imitate her in her obedience and service to You.*

MARCH 26
Walking by Faith

NOTHING is more counter to the spirit of the Gospel than to hunger after signs and wonders. The rule of Scripture interpretation now given is especially adapted to wean us from such wanderings of heart. It is our duty, rather it is our blessedness, to walk by faith.

Therefore we will take the promises in faith. We will believe they are fulfilled and enjoy the fruit of them before we see it. —*Glory of the Church*

PRAYER. *Holy Spirit of God, let me always rejoice in Your consolation, and let me walk by faith.*

MARCH 27
Existence of Things Invisible

THERE are two worlds, "the visible and the invisible," as the Creed speaks—the world we see, and the world we do not see. The world which we do not see exists as really as the world we do see.

This is that other world, which the eyes reach not, but faith only. He is there Who is above all beings, Who has created all, before Whom they all are as nothing, and with Whom nothing can be compared, Almighty God. —*Invisible World*

PRAYER. *Blessed Savior, while I go about my daily activities, help me to realize that I do not have on earth "an everlasting city."*

MARCH 28
Our Souls Are Immortal

IN the case of all, the soul, when severed from the body, returns to God. God gave it. He made it. He sent it into the body and He upholds it there. He upholds it in distinct existence, wherever it is. It animates the body while life lasts. It relapses into the unseen state upon death.

The point to be considered is this, that every soul which is or has been on earth has a separate existence, whether joined to a body or not.
—*Individuality of the Soul*

PRAYER. *Eternal Father, You created me and placed my soul in this mortal body. When this life passes, be merciful to me.*

MARCH 29
Fear To Sin against God's Grace

WE have had the Sign of the Cross set on us in infancy. It is our profession. We had the water poured on us. Let us fear to sin after grace given, lest a worse thing come upon us.

Let us aim at learning these two great truths: that we can do nothing good without God's grace, yet that we can sin against that grace. Thus, the great gift may be made the cause, on the one hand, of our gaining eternal life, and the occasion to us, on the other, of eternal misery.

—*Infant Baptism*

PRAYER. *Almighty God, may I never presume on Your mercy but always do my best to keep Your Commandments.*

MARCH 30
God's Judgment on Error

SCHISM, innovation in doctrine, a counterfeit priesthood, sacrilege, and violence, are sins so heinous that there is no judgment too great for them.

May God have pity upon our Church, rescue it from the dominion of the godless, and grant that the One Church Catholic may joyfully serve Him in all godly quietness! —*Jeroboam*

PRAYER. *Sovereign Lord, do not let the disobedience of certain religious leaders be a scandal to me. May I ever be guided by the Holy Father and the Bishops in union with him.*

MARCH 31
Christian Zeal

THE fire of zeal shows itself not by force and blood but as really and certainly as if it did. It cuts through natural feelings, neglecting self, preferring God's glory to all things. It firmly resists sin.

Zeal is a duty belonging to all creatures of God, a duty of Christians, in the midst of all that excellent overflowing charity which is the highest Gospel grace and the fulfilling of the second Commandment of the Law. —*Jewish Zeal, a Pattern*

PRAYER. *Blessed Lord, You showed us by Your example zeal for the things of God. Help me to cherish and to seek Your glory.*

APRIL 1
Remembering Good Friday

WE are near that most sacred day when we commemorate Christ's Passion and Death. Let us clear our minds of things temporal, and occupy them with the contemplation of the Eternal Priest and His one ever-enduring Sacrifice—that Sacrifice which, though completed once for all on Calvary, yet ever abides.

Let us look upon Him Who was lifted up that He might draw us to Him. —*Incarnate Son, a Sufferer*

PRAYER. *Dear Lord, we yearly recall the day You offered Yourself as a sacrifice for our sins. Help me keep in mind all You have done for me out of love.*

52

APRIL 2
Daily Mass and Communion

I T is our business to repent of our own sins and to try to escape from the disadvantages under which we find ourselves. Especially should we turn our thoughts to the consideration of the Mass and Holy Communion which since ancient times has been celebrated daily.

Is it not astonishing that we are so inconsistent and variable—when we will not seek of Him such daily sustenances of grace as He offers to us and when we do not pray to Him daily or seek His house daily?—*Judaism of the Present Day*

PRAYER. *My life, O Lord, does not allow me to participate at Mass every day. When I do, grant me a sincere appreciation of Your great gift.*

APRIL 3
Practicing What We Profess

O FTEN, men who have the Name of Christ in their mouths think they believe in Him, yet when trial comes, they are unable to act upon the principles which they profess.

They have thought that, since it is the Christian's duty to rejoice evermore, they would rejoice better if they never sorrowed. Let us be sure that as previous humiliation sobers our joy, it alone secures it.   —*Keeping Fast and Festival*

PRAYER. *Ever give me strength, O God, always to act in conformity with Your divine Revelation. Help me always to practice what I profess.*

APRIL 4
Christ Our Mediator

THE thing cannot be named in heaven or earth within the limits of truth which we cannot do through Christ. The petition cannot be named which may not be accorded to us for His Name's sake.

His infinite influence with the Father is ours. Not always to use, for perhaps it would not be good for us, but so fully ours, that when we ask and do things according to His will we are really possessed of a power with God and do prevail.
—*Keeping Fast and Festival*

PRAYER. *Almighty God, grant the petitions I make through Christ, if it is for my benefit.*

APRIL 5
God's Mercy for Jesus' Sake

REMEMBER me, O Lord, when You come into Your Kingdom" (Lk 23:42). Such was the prayer of the penitent thief on the cross, such must be our prayer. Who can do us any good but He?

We can say nothing to God in defense of ourselves but merely beg Him to bear us in mind in mercy, for His Son's sake. Even though we have served Him from our youth up, yet, at the very best, how much have we left undone, how much done, which ought to be otherwise! —*Lapse of Time*

PRAYER. *Ever gracious Savior, Your sacrifice on the Cross has redeemed the world and reconciled us to the Father. Have mercy on me.*

APRIL 6
Christ, Yesterday, Today, and Tomorrow

HE is not here, but is risen!" (Lk 24:6). These were words spoken so long ago, yet they hold good to this day. Christ is to us now, just what He was in all His glorious Attributes on the morning of the Resurrection.

And we are blessed in knowing it, even more than the women to whom the Angels spoke, according to His own assurance, "Blessed are they that have not seen, and yet have believed" (Jn 20:29). —*Christ, a Quickening Spirit*

PRAYER. Your Resurrection, my Jesus, has given me hope for my future resurrection and glory. Preserve me from all sin.

APRIL 7
Contentment with God's Gifts

WHEN Christians have but a little, they are thankful. They gladly pick up the crumbs from under the table. Give them much, they soon forget it is much.

Without denying in words their own unworthiness, they have a certain secret over-regard for themselves. At least they act as if they thought that the Christian privileges belonged to them over others by a sort of fitness.

—*Contracted Views in Religion*

PRAYER. Most blessed Father, may I always be content with the wonderful gifts You give me.

APRIL 8
Salvation through Jesus

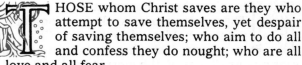

THOSE whom Christ saves are they who attempt to save themselves, yet despair of saving themselves; who aim to do all and confess they do nought; who are all love and all fear.

Those whom Christ enlightens understand that it is possible to work out their salvation, yet to have it wrought out for them, to tremble at the thought of judgment, yet to rejoice always in the Lord and hope and pray for His coming.

—*Lapse of Time*

PRAYER. *Blessed Mother of God and my Mother, pray for me that I may be worthy of the promises of your divine Son.*

APRIL 9
Faith, the Beginning of Salvation

FAITH is the element of all perfection. He who begins with faith will end in unspotted and entire holiness. It is the earnest of a great deal more than itself and therefore is allowed, in God's consideration, to stand for, to be a pledge of salvation.

Let us beg of God to lead us on in His perfect and narrow way and to be "a lantern to our feet and a light to our path" (Ps 119:105), while we walk in it. —*Law of the Spirit*

PRAYER. *God of all ages, Abraham, our father in faith, has given us an example of believing in Your promises. Help me to imitate him.*

APRIL 10
Persevering in God's Grace

PERSONS who persevere to the end will be perfect in soul and body when they stand before God in heaven. They will one day be presented blameless before the Throne, and they are now to labor toward and begin that perfect state.

And in consideration that it is begun in them, God of His great mercy anticipates what will be and treats them as that which they are laboring to become. —*Law of the Spirit*

PRAYER. Ever-loving Savior, never let me become discouraged in serving You. Help me to make daily progress in my spiritual life.

APRIL 11
Living a New Life with Christ

START now with this holy season and rise with Christ. See, He offers you His hand. He is rising. Rise with Him. Mount up from the grave of the old Adam, from groveling cares, and jealousies, and fretfulness, and worldly aims.

Rise from the tumult of passion, from the fascinations of the flesh, from a cold, worldly, calculating spirit, from frivolity, and from selfishness. Watch and pray and meditate.

—*Rising with Christ*

PRAYER. Your Resurrection, O Jesus, gives me hope for my future immortality. Let me live every day of my life in union with You.

APRIL 12
Salvation by Faith and Good Works

THERE can be no doubt at all that salvation is by faith. Still it may be by works also. To use a familiar illustration, obedience is the *road* to heaven and faith the *gate*.

Those who attempt to be saved simply without works are like persons who attempt to travel to a place, not along the road, but across the fields. If we wish to get to our journey's end, we shall keep to the road.—*New Works of the Gospel*

PRAYER. *Almighty God, You have told us that salvation depends on faith and good works. Help me to cooperate with Your grace in performing good works this day.*

APRIL 13
Life on Christian Principles

ET us love one another. Let us be meek and gentle; let us try to improve our talents; let us do good, not hoping for a return.

Well may I so exhort you when we have partaken of the Blessed Sacrament which binds us to mutual love, and gives us strength to practice it. We are not our own; we are bought with the Blood of Christ; we are consecrated to be temples of the Holy Spirit! —*Love of Relations*

PRAYER. *Almighty and merciful Lord, send me Your Holy Spirit and make me the temple of Your glory.*

APRIL 14
Sorrow for Sins

FOR those who have in any grievous way sinned or neglected God, I recommend such persons never to forget they *have* sinned. Let them every day, fall on their knees and say, "Lord, forgive me my past sins."

Let them look on all pain and sorrow as a *punishment* and take it patiently on that account, with a hope that God is punishing them here instead of hereafter. —*Life the Season of Repentance*

PRAYER. *Almighty God, I am sorry for all my sins. I hate them because they offend You, Who are all good and worthy of my love.*

APRIL 15
God's Saving Grace

WE never can guess what a man is by nature by seeing what self-discipline has made him. Yet if we do become thereby changed and prepared for heaven, it is no praise or merit to us. It is God's doing—glory be to Him, Who has dealt so wonderfully with us!

In heaven, sin will be utterly destroyed in every elect soul. We shall have our Savior's holiness fulfilled in us and be able to love God without drawback or infirmity.

—*Love of Religion*

PRAYER. *Dear Lord, keep me from sin by Your grace. Let me live for the day when I am joined to You in heaven.*

APRIL 16
Christ's Great Mercy toward Us

ET us dwell often upon Christ's manifold mercies to us: His adorable counsels, as manifested in our personal election; how it is that we are called and others not; the gifts He has given us; the answers He has accorded to our prayers.

Let us meditate upon His dealings with His Church; how He has ever led His people safely amid so many enemies.

—Love, the One Thing Needful

PRAYER. *O God, arouse in my heart lively sentiments of gratitude for Your great mercy toward me throughout my life.*

APRIL 17
Focusing on God

SUPPOSE the greater number of persons who try to live Christian lives are dissatisfied that the love of God, and of man for His sake, is not their ruling principle.

They may call themselves cold, or hard-hearted, but they mean that their affections do not rest on Almighty God as their great Object. Their reason and their heart do not go together. Their reason tends heavenward and their heart earthward. *—Love, the One Thing Needful*

PRAYER. *In spite of the distractions of this world, O Lord, assist me to be mindful of Your great love for me. Let me focus on You every day.*

APRIL 18
Living by God's Rules

GO where you will, you find persons with their own standards of right and wrong. Go where you will, you find certain persons held in esteem as patterns of what men should be.

Your perplexity in reconciling the surface of things with our Lord's announcements, the temptation to explain away the plain words of Scripture, shows you that your standard of good and evil, and the standard of all around you, must be very different from God's standard.

—*Many Called, Few Chosen*

PRAYER. *Heavenly Father, do not allow me to be influenced by the bad example of prominent people. Let me always try to serve You.*

APRIL 19
Perseverance in the Faith

THE doctrine that few are chosen though many be called should not make us fancy ourselves secure and others reprobate. We cannot see the heart, we can but judge from externals, from words and deeds, professions and habits.

But these will not save us, unless we persevere in them to the end. They count for nothing till they are completed.   —*Many Called, Few Chosen*

PRAYER. *Blessed Savior, do not allow me to become lazy in Your service. Give me the strength always to persevere.*

APRIL 20
Daily Sacrifices

WHAT are we but sinful dust and ashes, creeping on to heaven, not with any noble sacrifice for Christ's cause, but without pain, without trouble, in the midst of worldly blessings! But God can save even in the most tranquil times.

Let us strive to be more humble, faithful, merciful, meek, self-denying than we are. This, to be sure, is sorry martyrdom; yet God accepts it for His Son's sake. —*Martyrdom*

PRAYER. *Accept, O Lord, the small sacrifices I make each day. Enable me to glorify You by a devout and ordinary life.*

APRIL 21
Living in God's Presence

IS God habitually in our thoughts? Do we think of Him and of His Son our Savior through the day? When we eat and drink, do we thank Him, not as a mere matter of form but in spirit? When we do things in themselves right, do we lift up our minds to Him and desire to promote His glory?

In the exercise of our callings, do we still think of Him, desiring to know His will and aiming at fulfilling it more completely?

—*Mental Prayer*

PRAYER. *Dear Lord, amid the distractions of my daily life, help me to be mindful of Your abiding presence and support.*

APRIL 22
Become Little Children

RECOLLECT our Lord's impressive action and word, when He called a little child to Him, and said, "I say to you, unless you be converted, and become as little children, you shall not enter into the Kingdom of Heaven" (Mt 18:3).

There is very great danger of our being coldhearted, as life goes on. Afflictions which happen to us tend to blunt our affections and make our feelings callous. —*Mind of Little Children*

PRAYER. Dear Jesus, You welcomed little children and blessed them. As I grow older, never let me lose the characteristics of simple children.

APRIL 23
Effect of Venial Sins

SINGLE sins indulged or neglected are often the cause of other defects of character, which seem to have no connection with them. Wanderings in prayer may have some subtle connection with self-conceit; or passionateness may owe its power over us to indulgence in eating and drinking.

Who can pretend to estimate the effect of this apparently slight transgression upon the spiritual state of any one of us? —*Consequences of Single Sins*

PRAYER. Dear Lord, let me always be aware that my deliberate venial sins offend You and cause me to be careless in my duties.

APRIL 24
Pardon and Peace

WHAT a need we have of a cleansing and a restoration day by day! What a need we have of drawing near to God in faith and penitence, to seek from Him such pardon, such assurance, such strength, as He will bestow!

What a need we have to continue in His presence, to be steadfast in His Ordinances, and zealous in His precepts, lest we be found shelterless when He visits the earth!

—*Consequences of Single Sins*

PRAYER. *Allow me, O Lord, to draw near to You for pardon of my sins and give me assurance of Your forgiveness.*

APRIL 25
Following the Good Shepherd

THE sheep had no guide when Christ came in His infinite mercy "to gather in one the children of God that were scattered abroad" (Jn 11:52). Though for a moment, when in the conflict with the enemy the Good Shepherd had to lay down His life for the sheep, they were left without a guide, yet He soon rose from death to live for ever.

From that time the Good Shepherd has gone before them and "they follow the Lamb wherever He goes" (Rv 14:4). —*Shepherd of Our Souls*

PRAYER. *Lord Jesus, call me into Your sheepfold and keep me safe amid the troubles of life.*

APRIL 26
Believing Revealed Truth

I N matters such as Revealed Religion, surely it is most unwise to stumble at its mysteries, instead of believing and acting upon its promises. Instead of embracing what they can understand men criticize the wording in which truths are conveyed.

The Apostles taught and preserved them. And we, instead of rejoicing that they should have handed on to us those secrets concerning God, have hearts cold enough to complain of their mysteriousness. —*Mysteriousness of Our Being*

PRAYER. *Almighty God, I believe all that You have revealed and Your Church teaches. Help me to act in accordance with my belief.*

APRIL 27
Our Trust in the Savior

O UR Redeemer lives; He has been on earth and will come again. On Him we venture our all; we can bear thankfully to put ourselves into His hands, our interests present and eternal.

"Who shall separate us from His love? Shall tribulation, or distress, or persecution? No, in all these things, we are more than conquerors, through Him that loved us" (Rom 8:35-37).

—*Mysteries in Religion*

PRAYER. *Relying on Your infinite goodness and promises, O Lord, I hope to obtain pardon of my sins and life everlasting.*

APRIL 28

Christ Our Light

WE are in a world of mystery, with one bright Light before us, sufficient for our proceeding forward through all difficulties. Take away this Light, and we are utterly wretched—we know not where we are, how we are sustained, what will become of us, and of all that is dear to us, what we are to believe, and why we are in being.

But with it we have all and abound!

—Mysteries in Religion

PRAYER. *Without You, O Christ, I am in darkness. Enlighten me and let me see Your good and gracious purpose working in my life.*

APRIL 29

Mystery of the Blessed Trinity

LET us gain great benefit from the mystery of the Ever-blessed Trinity. It is calculated to humble the wise and elevate the lowly.

In the Beatific Vision of God we shall comprehend what we now desire to know. How the Father is truly and by Himself God, the Eternal Son truly and by Himself God, and the Holy Spirit truly and by Himself God, and yet not three Gods but one God.

—Mysteriousness of Our Being

PRAYER. *Eternal God, I thank You for giving us a glimpse of Your inner life in the mystery of the Trinity. May I dwell on this mystery every day.*

APRIL 30
Adopted Children of God

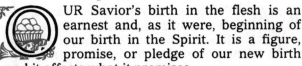UR Savior's birth in the flesh is an earnest and, as it were, beginning of our birth in the Spirit. It is a figure, promise, or pledge of our new birth and it effects what it promises.

As He is the Son of God by nature, so are we sons of God by grace. He is our Brother by virtue of His Incarnation and having sanctified our nature in Himself, He communicates it to us.

—Mystery of Godliness

PRAYER. *Most loving Father, now that I have become Your child through Baptism, help me always to live up to Your expectations.*

MAY 1
The Month of Mary

AY is the month of *promise* and of *hope.* It is the month that *begins* and heralds in the summer.

May is the month, if not of fulfillment, at least of *promise;* and is not this the very aspect in which we most suitably regard the Blessed Virgin? She was the sure *promise* of the coming Savior, and therefore May is by a special title her month.

—Meditations

PRAYER. *Dear Jesus, help me to give special honor to Your Holy Mother this month. For in doing so I will be honoring You and become close to You.*

MAY 2
A Month of Joy

MAY belongs to the Easter season, the time in which there are such frequent Alleluias, because Christ has risen from the grave. Here then we have a reason why May is dedicated to the Blessed Mary. She is the first of creatures, the most acceptable child of God, the dearest and nearest to Him.

It is fitting then that this month should be hers, in which we especially glory and rejoice in His great Providence to us. —*Meditations*

PRAYER. Heavenly Father, fill me with the joy of the Easter Season flowing from the Resurrection of Your Son. And let me worthily celebrate this month of Mary.

MAY 3
Virgin Most Pure

BY the Immaculate Conception of the Blessed Virgin is meant the revealed truth that she was conceived in the womb of her mother without original sin.

It was decreed, not that she should be *cleansed* from sin, but that she should, from the first moment of her being, be *preserved* from sin; so that the Evil One never had any part in her. —*Meditations*

PRAYER. Blessed Lord, inspire me to pray often to Your Mother: "O Mary, conceived without original sin, pray for us who have recourse to you."

MAY 4
Virgin Most Renowned

MARY is the *Virgin Most Renowned*, that is, the Virgin who is to be proclaimed, to be heralded; literally, to be *preached*.

First she was preached as the Virgin of Virgins—then as the Mother of God—then as glorious in her Assumption—then as the Advocate of sinners—then as Immaculate in her Conception. And this last has been the special preaching of the present century. —*Meditations*

PRAYER. *O God, teach me to proclaim the greatness of the Blessed Virgin to others. Let me daily spread the word about devotion to her.*

MAY 5
Mother Most Admirable

WHEN Mary, the *Mother Most Renowned*, the Virgin who is to be proclaimed aloud, is called by the title of *Admirable*, it is thereby suggested to us what the *effect* is of the preaching of her as Immaculate in her Conception.

The Holy Church proclaims, preaches her, as conceived without original sin; and those who hear, the children of Holy Church, wonder, marvel, are astonished and overcome by the preaching. It is so great a prerogative. —*Meditations*

PRAYER. *O Jesus, help me to imitate the purity of Your Holy Mother. Amid the pressing duties of daily life, keep me from all kinds of sin.*

MAY 6
House of Gold

MARY is called *golden* because her graces, her virtues, are of dazzling perfection, so exquisite that the Angels cannot, so to say, keep their eyes off her any more than we could help gazing upon any great work of gold.

She is the *house* and the *palace* of the Great King, of God Himself. Our Lord, the Coequal Son of God, once dwelt in her.　　*—Meditations*

PRAYER. *Lord Jesus, You told us to live in You and You would dwell in us. Help me to strive to avoid sin so that my soul may be a "house of gold" in which You are happy to dwell.*

MAY 7
Mother Most Lovable

OUR Lady's holiness was such that if we saw and heard her, we should not be able to tell anything about her except that she was angelic and heavenly.

There was a divine music in all she said and did—in her air, her deportment, that charmed every heart. Her innocence, her humility, her unaffected interest in everyone who came to her—these qualities made her so lovable.

—Meditations

PRAYER. *Jesus, my God, grant that I may be inspired by the lovable character of Your Holy Mother. Help me to be gracious to all those with whom I come into contact this day.*

MAY 8
Virgin Most Venerable

PEOPLE use the word *"Venerable"* generally of what is *old*. That is because only what is old has those qualities which excite reverence or veneration. It is a great history, a great character, a maturity of virtue, that excite our reverence.

Mary's prerogatives are such as to lead us to exclaim with exultation, "You are the glory of Jerusalem and the joy of Israel; you are the honor of our people" (Jdt 15:9).   —*Meditations*

PRAYER. *Lord, You made Mary the glory of Jerusalem and the joy of Israel. Help me to venerate her as the honor of the Christian people.*

MAY 9
Holy Mary

WHEN God would prepare a human mother for His Son, He began, not by giving her the gift of love, or truthfulness, or gentleness, or devotion, though according to the occasion she had them all. But He began by making her *holy*.

Mary in this way resembles her Son. As He, being God, is separate by holiness from all creatures, so she is separate from all Saints and Angels, as being *"full of grace."*   —*Meditations*

PRAYER. *Dear Jesus, grant that I may prize the gift of Your grace above all else. Let me imitate Your mother and strive to remain in Your grace all my life.*

MAY 10
Queen of Angels

THIS great title may be fitly connected with the Maternity of Mary, that is, with the coming upon her of the Holy Spirit at Nazareth after the Angel Gabriel's annunciation to her, and with the consequent birth of our Lord at Bethlehem. She, as the Mother of our Lord, comes nearer to Him than any Angel.

Now, as then, the Blessed Mother of God has hosts of Angels who do her service; and she is their Queen. —*Meditations*

PRAYER. *Almighty God, You have made the Blessed Virgin Mary Queen of the Angels. Help me to honor her and seek her intercession.*

MAY 11
Mirror of Justice

WHEN our Lady is called the "Mirror of Justice," it is meant to say that she is the Mirror of sanctity, holiness, supernatural goodness.

What is meant by calling her a *mirror*? A mirror is a surface which reflects. What did Mary reflect? She reflected our Lord—but *He is* infinite *Sanctity.* She then, as far as a creature could, reflected His Divine sanctity.

—*Meditations*

PRAYER. *God of holiness, teach me to go to Jesus through Mary. Let me realize that by imitating the virtues of the Mother of God, I imitate the virtues of Your Divine Son.*

MAY 12
Seat of Wisdom

MARY has the title *Seat of Wisdom* in her Litany because the Son of God, Who is also called in Scripture the Word and Wisdom of God, once dwelt in her and because of the knowledge which she gained from His conversation.

In her knowledge of the universe, Mary must have excelled the greatest of philosophers, and in her theological knowledge the greatest of theologians, and in her prophetic discernment the most favored of prophets. —*Meditations*

PRAYER. *Lord Jesus, enable me to strive for true wisdom rather than the wisdom of the world. Let me seek the wisdom found in Your Mother.*

MAY 13
Gate of Heaven

OUR Lady is called the *Gate* of Heaven, because it was through her that our Lord passed from heaven to earth. Ezekiel, prophesying of Mary, says, "No man shall pass through the gate, since God has entered through it—and it shall be closed for the Prince shall sit in it" (Ez 44:2-3).

Now this is fulfilled, not only in our Lord having taken flesh from her, but in that she had a place in the Redemption. —*Meditations*

PRAYER. *Almighty God, Mary is the Gate of Heaven. Through her help may I receive the fruits of the Redemption in life and in eternity.*

MAY 14
Mother of Our Creator

CHRISTIANS were accustomed from the first to call the Blessed Virgin "The Mother of God," because it was impossible to deny her that title without denying St. John's words, "The Word" (that is, God the Son) "was made flesh" (Jn 1:14).

And wonderful promises follow from this truth. If we live well, we shall be taken up by our Incarnate God to that place where Angels dwell.
—*Meditations*

PRAYER. Dear Jesus, through You the world and everything in it was created. By my devotion to Your Holy Mother, keep me united with You.

MAY 15
Mother of Christ

WHAT is the force of addressing Mary as the "Mother of Christ"? It is to bring before us that she it is who from the first was prophesied of, and associated with the hopes and prayers of all true worshipers of God, of all who "looked for the Redemption of Israel" (Lk 2:38).

Therefore we give praise to God the Holy Spirit, through Whom she was *both* Virgin *and* Mother.
—*Meditations*

PRAYER. Lord Jesus, You are the Messiah, our Redeemer. Through the prayers of Your Holy Mother, apply Your Redemption to the whole world this coming day.

MAY 16
Mother of the Savior

UR Lord was known before His coming as the Messiah, or Christ. But when He actually came, He was known by three new titles: the Son of God, the Son of Man, and the Savior; the first expressive of His Divine Nature, the second of His Human, the third of His Personal Office.

Certainly He came, not simply to be the Son of Mary, but to be the Savior of Man. —*Meditations*

PRAYER. *Almighty God, You made the Blessed Virgin the Mother of the Savior. Through her prayers, grant that all people may cooperate with Your grace and be saved.*

MAY 17
Queen of Martyrs

WHAT an overwhelming horror it must have been for the Blessed Mary to witness the Passion and the Crucifixion of her Son!

If our Lord Himself could not bear the prospect of what was before Him, and was covered in the thought of it with a bloody sweat, His soul thus acting upon His body, does not this show how great mental pain can be? Thus is Mary truly the Queen of Martyrs. —*Meditations*

PRAYER. *Heavenly Father, You bestowed on Mary a spiritual martyrdom. Enable me, through her prayers, to accept all the trials that are necessary for me to attain salvation.*

MAY 18
Singular Vessel of Devotion

INTENSE devotion toward our Lord, forgetting self, in love for Him, is instanced in the Blessed Virgin. When He was mocked, scourged, and nailed to the Cross, she felt as keenly as if every indignity and torture inflicted on Him was struck at herself.

This is called her *compassion*, or her suffering with her Son, and it arose from this that she was the "Singular Vessel of *Devotion*." —*Meditations*

PRAYER. *Dear Jesus, grant me to have true devotion toward You and Your Holy Mother. I offer everything for Your greater honor and glory.*

MAY 19
Vessel of Honor

ST. Paul calls elect souls vessels of honor: of honor, because they are elect or chosen; and vessels, because, through the love of God, they are filled with God's heavenly and holy grace. How much more then is Mary a vessel of honor by reason of her having within her, not only the grace of God, but the very Son of God, formed as regards His flesh and blood out of her!

Mary was a martyr without the rude *dishonor* which accompanied the sufferings of martyrs.
  —*Meditations*

PRAYER. *Lord Jesus, make me a vessel of honor after the example of Your Holy Mother. Enable me to be holy and come to dwell in my soul.*

MAY 20
Spiritual Vessel

TO be spiritual is to live in the world of spirits—as St. Paul says, "Our conversation is in heaven" (Phil 3:20). To be *spiritually* minded is to see by faith all those holy beings who actually surround us, though we see them not with our bodily eyes.

These visions consoled and strengthened the Blessed Virgin in all her sorrows. —*Meditations*

PRAYER. Almighty God, grant that I may be spiritually minded in imitation of the Blessed Virgin. Let me put my spiritual life before all else.

MAY 21
Comforter of the Afflicted

PERSONS able to comfort others are those who have been much tried, and have felt the need of consolation, and have received it.

And this too is why the Blessed Virgin is the comforter of the afflicted. We all know how special a mother's consolation is, and we are allowed to call Mary our Mother from the time that our Lord from the Cross established this relation. And she especially can console us because she suffered more than mothers in general. —*Meditations*

PRAYER. Dear Jesus, Your Holy Mother comforted You in Your earthly afflictions. In my afflictions, let me have recourse to her as the Comforter of the Afflicted.

MAY 22
Virgin Most Prudent

MARY'S life was full of duties—and in consequence she was full of merit. All her acts were the best that could be done. Now, always to be awake, guarded, fervent, so as to be able to act not only without sin, but in the best possible way, denotes a life of untiring mindfulness.

But of such a life, prudence is the presiding virtue. It is, then, through the pains and sorrows of her earthly pilgrimage that we are able to invoke her as *Virgin Most Prudent.* —*Meditations*

PRAYER. *Divine Master, let me follow the example given by Your Holy Mother. Enable me to practice the virtue of prudence every single day.*

MAY 23
Tower of Ivory

IN her magnanimity and generosity in suffering Mary is, as compared with the Apostles, fitly imaged as a *Tower.* But towers are huge, rough, graceless structures, with nothing of the beautifulness, refinement, and finish which are conspicuous in Mary.

Therefore, she is called the Tower of *Ivory,* to suggest to us, by the purity and exquisiteness of that material, how transcendent is the loveliness of the Mother of God. —*Meditations*

PRAYER. *Almighty God, You raised up the Blessed Virgin as a tower of generosity. Teach me to be magnanimous and generous to others.*

MAY 24
Holy Mother of God

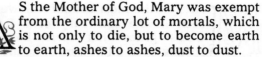

AS the Mother of God, Mary was exempt from the ordinary lot of mortals, which is not only to die, but to become earth to earth, ashes to ashes, dust to dust.

Although her body was for a while separated from her soul and consigned to the tomb, yet it did not remain there, but was speedily united to her soul again, and raised by our Lord to a new and eternal life of heavenly glory. —*Meditations*

PRAYER. *Lord Jesus, You assumed Your Holy Mother into heaven after her death. Grant that, after my death, I too may join You in heaven.*

MAY 25
Mother Undefiled

ONE reason for believing in our Lady's Assumption is that her Son loved her too much to let her body remain in the grave. A second reason is that she was not only dear to our Lord as a mother to a son but also so transcendently holy.

What had Mary done to forfeit the privilege given to our first parents in the beginning? Was her comeliness to be turned into corruption, without reason assigned? Impossible.

—*Meditations*

PRAYER. *Almighty God, You decreed that the sinless Mary should not suffer defilement in the grave. Through her prayers, forgive me for the times that I have sinned.*

MAY 26
Mystical Rose

MARY is the most beautiful flower ever seen in the spiritual world. It is by God's grace that there have ever sprung up at all flowers of holiness and glory. And Mary is the Queen of them. Therefore she is called the *Rose*, for the rose is of all flowers the most beautiful.

But moreover, she is the *Mystical,* or *hidden* Rose; for mystical means hidden. How is she now "hidden" from us? Her body was taken into heaven. —*Meditations*

PRAYER. *Almighty God, Mary was Your most beautiful flower. Grant me the grace to admire her beauty and to follow her inspirations.*

MAY 27
Tower of David

A TOWER in its simplest idea is a fabric for defense against enemies. David, King of Israel, built for this purpose a notable tower; and as he is a figure or type of our Lord, so is his tower a figure denoting our Lord's Virgin Mother.

She is called the *Tower* of David because she had so signally defended her Divine Son from the assaults of His foes. —*Meditations*

PRAYER. *Dear Jesus, Your Holy Mother defended You against the assaults of the enemy. Through her prayers, keep me safe from the attacks of the devil.*

MAY 28
Virgin Most Powerful

THE Blessed Virgin is called *Powerful*—nay sometimes, *All*-powerful, because she has, more than anyone else, more than all Angels and Saints, this great, prevailing gift of prayer. No one has access to the Almighty as His Mother has; none has merit such as hers. Her Son will deny her nothing that she asks; and herein lies her power.

While she defends the Church, neither men nor evil spirits can avail to harm us.—*Meditations*

PRAYER. *Lord Jesus, if You are with me, no one can take me away from You. Through the prayers of Your Holy Mother, defend Your Church amid the storms of the world.*

MAY 29
Help of Christians

OUR glorious Queen, since her Assumption on high, has been the minister of numberless services to the elect people of God upon earth, and to His Holy Church.

This title of "Help of Christians" relates to those services of which the Divine Office, while recording and referring to the occasion on which it was given her, recounts five, connecting them more or less with the Rosary.   —*Meditations*

PRAYER. *Dear Jesus, Your Mother is the Help of Christians. Through her prayers, keep all Christians safe this day from the powers of evil.*

MAY 30
Virgin Most Faithful

THE word *faithfulness* means loyalty to a superior, or exactness in fulfilling an engagement. Mary is preeminently faithful to her Lord and Son. Let no one for an instant suppose that she is not supremely zealous for His honor.

Her true servants are still more truly His. As He is zealous for her honor, so is she for His. He is the Fount of grace, and all her gifts are from His goodness. —*Meditations*

PRAYER. *Almighty God, Mary is the faithful Virgin, for she remained ever united with You and her Son. Grant that I may be faithful to You.*

MAY 31
Morning Star

IT is Mary's prerogative to be the *Morning Star* which heralds in the sun. She does not shine for herself, but she is the reflection of her and our Redeemer, and she glorifies *Him*. When she appears in the darkness, we know that He is close at hand.

He is Alpha and Omega, the First and the Last, the Beginning and the End. Behold He comes quickly, and His reward is with Him, to render to everyone according to his works. —*Meditations*

PRAYER. *Dear Jesus, help me to keep my eyes fixed on Mary, for she is the Morning Star who dispels darkness. May I have the grace to reach You through her.*

JUNE 1
New Creatures in Christ

ET us beware of dead works. Let us pray to be filled with the spirit of love. Let us come to church joyfully. Let us partake of Holy Communion adoringly.

Let us pray sincerely. Let us work cheerfully. Let us suffer thankfully. Let us throw our heart into all we think, say, and do, and may it be a spiritual heart! This is to be a new creature in Christ. —*New Works of the Gospel*

PRAYER. *Dear Lord, give me joy in serving You and in keeping Your Commandments. Help me to live as a new person in Christ.*

JUNE 2
Sufficiency of God's Grace

E should think much and make much of the grace of God. Let us beware of receiving it in vain. Let us pray God to prosper it in our hearts, that we may bring forth much fruit.

We see how grace worked in St. Paul. It made him labor, suffer, and work righteousness almost above man's nature. This was not through his own power but the grace of God. God's grace made him quite another man from what he was before. May God's grace be efficacious in us also. —*New Works of the Gospel*

PRAYER. *Blessed Savior, by Your grace You have made it possible for me to overcome the trials of this life. Help me to please You in all that I do.*

JUNE 3
God's Gift of the Spirit

 UCH is the inhabitation of the Holy Spirit within us, applying to us individually the precious cleansing of Christ's Blood in all its manifold benefits.

The heavenly gift of the Spirit fixes the eyes of our mind upon the Divine Author of our salvation. By nature we are blind and carnal; but the Holy Spirit, by Whom we are newborn, reveals to us the God of mercies and bids us recognize and adore Him as our Father. —*Indwelling Spirit*

PRAYER. *Dear Lord, let me always be aware that I am not to be attracted to the things of this world but to keep heaven as my goal.*

JUNE 4
The Life-giving Spirit

HE condescension of the Blessed Spirit is as incomprehensible as that of the Son. He has ever been the secret Presence of God within the Creation: a source of life amid the chaos, the voice of Truth in the hearts of all rational beings.

Hence He is especially called the "life-giving" Spirit; being (as it were) the Soul of universal nature, the Strength of man and beast, the Grace abiding in the Christian soul, and the Lord and Ruler of the Church. —*Indwelling Spirit*

PRAYER. *Let me ever praise the Father Who is the first Source of all perfection in and together with His Co-equal Son and Spirit.*

JUNE 5

The Church—Human and Divine

L ET us beware of supposing that, because Christ's Kingdom is not based upon this world, the Church is not connected with it.

Surely it was established here for the sake of this world, and must ever act in it, as if a part of it, though its origin is from above. Like the Angels which appeared to the Patriarchs, it is a Heavenly Messenger in human form.

—Christian Zeal

PRAYER. *Heavenly Father, Your Son has given us the Church to guide us through life. Let me always be attentive to her teachings.*

JUNE 6

The Church Is Our Light

T HIS we know for our comfort. Our light shall never go down; Christ set it upon a hill, and hell shall not prevail against it.

The Church will witness on to the last for the Truth, chained indeed to this world, but ever foretelling its ruin, though not believed, and in the end promised a far different recompense. For in the end the Lord Omnipotent shall reign.

—Profession without Ostentation

PRAYER. *Help me, O God, to listen to the voice of Your Church, even when I find it difficult to do so. Let me strive each day to be in tune with the Church.*

85

JUNE 7
God Knows Us Intimately

MEN would be overpowered by despondency and would even loathe existence did they suppose themselves under the mere operation of fixed laws, powerless to excite the pity or the attention of Him Who has appointed them.

The Gospel narrative supplies our very need, not simply presenting to us an unchangeable Creator to rely upon but a compassionate Guardian and Helper. God beholds you individually whoever you are. —*A Particular Providence*

PRAYER. *Blessed Jesus, You told us that God knows even when a sparrow falls. Help me to realize how much more He regards me.*

JUNE 8
God's Particular Providence

IT is very difficult, in spite of the revelation made to us in the Gospel, to master the idea of the particular providence of God.

We conceive that Almighty God works on a large plan. But we cannot realize the wonderful truth that He sees and thinks of individuals. We cannot believe He is really present everywhere, that He is wherever we are, though unseen. We know He is in heaven and forget that He is also on earth. —*A Particular Providence*

PRAYER. *Your presence and knowledge, O God, extend to all creation. Help me to be aware of You in every circumstance of life.*

JUNE 9
Trusting in God

TRUST in God is a sentiment which often occurs in Scripture whether expressed in words or implied in the conduct of good men. It is founded on the belief that God is our sole strength, our sole refuge.

If good is in any way in store for us, it lies with God. If it is attainable it is attained by coming to God.

—Peace amid Chastisement

PRAYER. *O my God, relying on Your infinite goodness and promises, I hope to obtain pardon of my sins, the help of Your grace and life everlasting.*

JUNE 10
Praying for Gospel Virtues

LET us beg God to give us an understanding heart, and that love of Him which is the instinct of the new creature and the breath of spiritual life. Let us pray for the spirit of obedience, of true dutifulness, an honest spirit, earnestly set to do His will, with no selfish designs of our own, no preferences of the creature to the Creator.

So will He, as time goes on, take up His abode in us.

—Peace in Believing

PRAYER. *Grant me, O Lord, the grace to practice the virtues You exemplified while You were here on earth.*

JUNE 11
Conscience Is Our Guide

BEWARE of trifling with your conscience. It is often said that second thoughts are best; so they are in matters of judgment, but not in matters of conscience.

In matters of duty first thoughts are commonly best—they have more in them of the voice of God. May He give you grace to hear what has been said, to hear in a practical way, with a desire to profit by it, to learn God's will, and to do it!
—*Obedience without Love*

PRAYER. Ever-living Lord, prompt me by Your grace to know what I should do and grant me the help to do it.

JUNE 12
God's Gift of the Old Testament

WHEN we consider the Old Testament as written by divine inspiration, and preserved, beyond the time of its own dispensation, for us Christians, we ought not to read any portion of it with indifference, nay without great and anxious interest.

Christ and His Apostles cannot have put the Law and the Prophets into our hands for nothing.
—*Obedience without Love*

PRAYER. You have given me, my God, the Bible as a source of Your revelation. Help me to understand and treasure the Old Testament as well as the New.

JUNE 13
Living Life Wisely

IT is plainly our duty to make the most of our time; to do all we can to please God; to endeavor to bring to fruit the gifts of His grace within us.

He at present condescends to work in us "to will and to do" (Phil 2:13), to aim as St. Paul directs, at "working out our own salvation with fear and trembling" (Phil 2:12), for "now is the acceptable time" (2 Cor 2:3).

—*Peace amid Chastisement*

PRAYER. *Dear Lord, whether my time on earth is long or short, let me use it for Your honor and glory. Help me to get closer to You each day.*

JUNE 14
Christian Soldiers on the March

THE Church is rising up around us day by day toward heaven and we do nothing but object, or criticize, or make excuses, or wonder. Oh, may we be loyal and affectionate before our race is run!

Let us take up our cross and follow Christ. Let us take to us "the whole armor of God, that we may be able to stand against the wiles of the devil" (Eph 6:11).

—*Power of the Will*

PRAYER. *Dear Jesus, You left Your Church to guide us to heaven. Help me to follow You in all things and thus be a loyal member of that Church.*

89

JUNE 15
Our Faith Leads to Action

WHILE we think of God, let us not forget to be up and doing. Let us beware of indulging a mere barren faith and love, which dreams instead of working and is fastidious when it should be hardy. This is only spiritual childhood in another form.

The Holy Spirit is the Author of active good works and leads us to the observance of all lowly deeds of ordinary obedience as the most pleasing sacrifice to God. —*Christian Manhood*

PRAYER. *O God, grant me the assistance to be a "doer" and not a dreamer. May Your Holy Spirit lead me to carry out active good works.*

JUNE 16
Worship of the Heart

GOD hates the worship of the mere lips; He requires the worship of the heart. A person may bow, and kneel, and look religious, but he is not at all the nearer heaven, unless he tries to obey God in all things.

If he does so, then his outward manner will be reverent also; decent forms will become natural to him; holy ordinances, though coming to him from the Church, will at the same time come (as it were) from his heart. —*Reverence in Worship*

PRAYER. *Dear God, I cannot always think of You or picture You in my imagination. But teach me to have my heart always focused on You.*

JUNE 17
Seizing the Moment

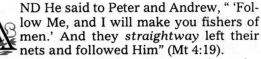

ND He said to Peter and Andrew, " 'Follow Me, and I will make you fishers of men.' And they *straightway* left their nets and followed Him" (Mt 4:19).

Others who seemed to waver, or rather who asked for some little delay from human feeling, were rebuked for want of promptitude in their obedience—for time stays for no one; the word of call is spoken and is gone; if we do not seize the moment, it is lost. —*Divine Calls*

PRAYER. *Dear Jesus, Your call comes to us in various ways and at different times. Help me to seize the moment when You call and never waver in following Your word.*

JUNE 18
Freedom To Practice Our Religion

ET us bless and praise God for the present peace of the Church and the freedom of speech and action which He has vouchsafed to us. There have been times when to be a Christian was to be an outcast and a criminal.

We have large and noble churches to worship in. We go freely to worship when we will; we may speak our mind; we may write what we will—without suffering or inconvenience.

—*Present Blessings*

PRAYER. *Ever-loving Savior, may Your Church continue to be granted freedom to spread Your Gospel everywhere in the world.*

JUNE 19
The Great Gifts of God

HOW great is our privilege of daily Mass and Communion. How pleasant to come, day after day, quietly and calmly, to kneel before our Maker, and to meet our Lord and Savior.

He, the Lord of glory, stands over us and comes down upon us and gives Himself to us. He pours forth milk and honey for our sustenance, though we see Him not. Surely we have everything! —*Present Blessings*

PRAYER. *Help me to appreciate the great privilege of Mass and Communion, O Lord. Never allow me to take for granted these great gifts.*

JUNE 20
The Sentiments of a Christian

GLOOM is not a Christian sentiment. That repentance is not real which has not love in it. That self-chastisement is not acceptable which is not sweetened by faith and cheerfulness.

We must live in sunshine, even when we sorrow. We must live in God's presence. We must not shut ourselves up in our own hearts, even when we are reckoning up our past sins. If God then gives us grace to repent, it is well.

—*Present Blessings*

PRAYER. *Grant me, O Lord, ever to rejoice in the consolation that Your forgiveness brings. Let me rejoice in Your presence in me.*

JUNE 21
Avoiding Hypocrisy

T is surely most necessary to beware, as our Lord solemnly bids us, of the leaven of the Pharisees, which is hypocrisy. We may be infected with it, even though we are not conscious of our insincerity.

I would maintain that no one is to be reckoned a Pharisee or hypocrite in his prayers who *tries* not to be one—who aims at knowing and correcting himself—and who is accustomed to pray, though not perfectly, yet not indolently or in a self-satisfied way. —*Profession without Hypocrisy*

PRAYER. *Dearest Lord, help me to know Your truth so that I may attain to it by a worthy life. Assist me to seek You sincerely.*

JUNE 22
Disposing Ourselves To Pray

HEN we pray let us not be as the hypocrites, making a show; nor use vain repetitions.

Let us compose ourselves, and kneel down quietly as to a work far above us, preparing our minds for our own imperfection in prayer, meekly repeating the wonderful words of the Church our Teacher, and desiring with the Angels to look into them.

—*Profession without Hypocrisy*

PRAYER. *O Lord, help me to be recollected and composed when I come before You to pray. Teach me the art of prayer.*

93

JUNE 23
Conforming Oneself to Christ

ET us endeavor to enter more and more fully into the meaning of our prayers and professions; let us humble ourselves for the very little we do, and the poor advance we make; let us do our duty in that state of life to which God has called us.

Thus, we shall, through God's grace, form within us the mind of Christ. We shall be the image of Him Who died that we might be conformed to His likeness. —*Profession without Hypocrisy*

PRAYER. *O God, let me be conformed to Christ. May my mind be on doing Your will and the reward You have promised to those who serve You.*

JUNE 24
God's Invitation To Pray

OD accepts those who come in faith, bringing nothing as their offering but a confession of sin.

This is the highest excellence to which we ordinarily attain; to understand our own hypocrisy, insincerity, and shallowness of mind; to admit, while we pray, that we cannot pray aright; and to submit ourselves wholly to His judgment, Who could indeed be extreme with us, but has already shown His loving-kindness in bidding us to pray. —*Profession without Hypocrisy*

PRAYER. *Receive, O Lord, I ask You, my pious acts of devotion. Purify my intentions and dispositions so that I may one day attain heaven.*

94

JUNE 25
Christ Displayed in Our Life

CONSIDER how great a profession of faith, and yet a profession how unconscious and modest, arises from the mere ordinary manner in which any strict Christian lives. Let this thought be a satisfaction to uneasy minds which fear lest they are not confessing Christ, yet dread to display.

Your *life* displays Christ without your intending it. You cannot help it. Your *words and deeds* will show in the long run where your treasure is, and your heart.   —*Profession without Ostentation*

PRAYER. *Father in heaven, help me spread Your fragrance everywhere. Let my life be a reflection of the teaching of Christ, my Savior.*

JUNE 26
God, the Final Judge

DELUSION may come upon you, if you forget that you are hereafter to be tried one by one at God's judgment-seat, according to your works.

Let us consider whether we should act as strictly as we now do were the eyes of our acquaintances and neighbors withdrawn from us. What I am asking you is not whether you merely regard man's opinion, but whether you set it before God's judgment.   —*Profession without Practice*

PRAYER. *Grant, O Lord, that I may be preserved from the dangers of this life and arrive at everlasting life with You and Your Saints.*

95

JUNE 27
Deceiving Ourselves and Others

THIS then is hypocrisy, not simply for a man to deceive others, knowing all the while that he *is* deceiving them, but to deceive himself *and* others at the same time; to aim at their praise by a religious profession, without perceiving that he loves their praise more than the praise of God, and that he is professing far more than he practices.

And if this be the true Scripture meaning of the word, we have some insight into the reasons which induced our Divine Teacher to warn His Disciples in so marked a way against hypocrisy.

—*Profession without Practice*

PRAYER. *Almighty God, You are all truth. Grant me the grace to serve You in sincerity and truth.*

JUNE 28
Humility in Our Life

WHETHER rich or poor, learned or unlearned, walking by the rule of humility we shall become, at length, true Saints, sons of God.

We shall be upright and perfect, lights in the world, the image of Him Who died that we might be conformed to His likeness.

—*Profession without Hypocrisy*

PRAYER. *Teach me to be humble, O Lord. And let me be a light in the world by walking humbly in Your way.*

JUNE 29
Evidence of True Faith

HE who does one little deed of obedience, whether he denies himself some comfort or forgives an enemy, evinces more true faith than could be shown by the most fluent religious conversation, or the most intimate knowledge of Scripture.

Yet how many are there who sit still with folded hands, dreaming, thinking they have done everything, when they merely have had these good *thoughts* which will save no one!

—Promising without Doing

PRAYER. *Infuse, O Lord, in my heart the vigor of Your grace so that I may give evidence of my faith by putting it into action.*

JUNE 30
Knowledge of Self

MY object has been to lead you to some true notion of the deceitfulness of the heart, which we do not really know. It is easy to speak of human nature as corrupt in general, and to admit it in general.

But in truth we can have no real apprehension of our corruption till we view the structure of our minds, part by part, and dwell upon and draw out the signs of our weakness and inconsistency.

—Promising without Doing

PRAYER. *Almighty God, grant me a true knowledge of myself so that I may serve You with sincerity.*

JULY 1
Fraternal Correction

AIM at viewing all things in a plain and candid light, and at calling them by their right names. Be frank, do not keep your notions of right and wrong to yourselves. Do not allow friend or stranger to advance false opinions, nor shrink from stating your own, and do this in singleness of mind and love.

We daily influence each other for good or evil; let us not be the occasion of misleading others by our silence, when we ought to speak.

—*Rebuking Sin*

PRAYER. *Keep me mindful, O Lord, that while I can see very clearly the faults of others, I cannot ignore my own.*

JULY 2
Our Goodness Due to God's Grace

THERE can be no boasting, because whatever we do is the fruit of God's grace, and we do very little. Even if we did all, we should be doing no more than we are bound to do.

There are many persons in the world who are well pleased with what they are and what they do, who are what is commonly called self-righteous.

—*Reliance on Observances*

PRAYER. *Let me always rely on Your grace, O Lord, to accomplish whatever good I do and thereby give You glory.*

JULY 3
Curiosity—a Temptation to Sin

O NE chief cause of the wickedness which is everywhere seen in the world is our curiosity to have some experience of sin. Not to know sin by experience brings upon a man the laughter and jests of his companions; nor is it astonishing this should be the case in the descendants of that guilty pair to whom Satan in the beginning held out admittance into a strange world of knowledge and enjoyment as the reward of disobedience to God's Commandment. —*Curiosity a Temptation*

PRAYER. *Dear Jesus, teach me to set aside foolish curiosity and to strive especially for knowledge that will help me to know and love You more.*

JULY 4
Joining Our Suffering to Christ's

L ET us compose ourselves and bear a firm and courageous heart. Let us steel ourselves not against self-reproach and self-hatred but against fear. Let us feel what we really are—sinners who are willing to take their part with Christ, in suffering as in joy.

Trials in the present world are recompensed by the faith, humility, patience, and gentleness resulting from them. —*Reliance on Observances*

PRAYER. *Receive, O Lord, the offering of my fears and anxieties. Let me feel Your comfort through prayer and the Sacraments.*

JULY 5
Obedience Leads to Heaven

GOD has promised to lead us safely heavenward in spite of all things being against us. But the infirmities which beset us, these He still ordains should try us and humble us and should bring us day by day to the foot of His Cross for pardon.

Let us simply obey God's will whatever may befall us. He can turn all things to our eternal good. He can bless and sanctify even our infirmities. —*Reliance on Observances*

PRAYER. Dear Jesus, ever assist me, by Your grace, to accept whatever hardships come my way. For they will lead me to You.

JULY 6
A House of Prayer

IN church, we must in all respects act as if we saw God; that is, if we believe that God is here, we shall keep silence; we shall not laugh, or talk, or whisper during the Service, as many young persons do; we shall not gaze about us.

We shall follow the example set us by the Church itself. I mean, as the words in which we pray in church are not our own, neither will our looks, or our postures, or our thoughts, be our own. —*Reverence in Worship*

PRAYER. Dear Jesus, You said that Your Father's house, the church, was a house of prayer. Let my words and actions there be always reverent.

JULY 7
Self-righteousness

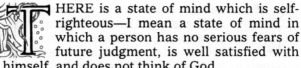HERE is a state of mind which is self-righteous—I mean a state of mind in which a person has no serious fears of future judgment, is well satisfied with himself, and does not think of God.

Self-righteous men have no fears for the future. They are contented with themselves, because they live in what is visible and tangible and do not measure themselves by what is unseen and spiritual. —*Reliance on Observances*

PRAYER. *Heavenly Father, help me to know myself as I really am. Do not let me pretend to be more than I am.*

JULY 8
Possess Your Souls in Peace

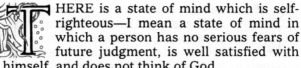OW long and earnestly must you pray, how many years must you pass in careful obedience, before you have any right to lay aside sorrow, and to rejoice in the Lord?

You may take comfort from the first; for you know He desires your salvation. has died for you, has washed away your sins by Baptism, and will ever help you. This thought must cheer you while you turn to God in self-denial.

—*Religion of the Day*

PRAYER. *Pour down on me, O Lord, the Spirit of Your love and grant that I may serve You with joy and in peace.*

JULY 9
Relying on God

YOU never can be sure of salvation while you are here; and therefore you must always fear while you hope.

This is the true Christian state, a deep resignation to God's will, a surrender of ourselves, soul and body, to Him; hoping, indeed, that we shall be saved, but fixing our eyes more earnestly on Him than on ourselves; that is, acting for His glory, seeking to please Him, devoting ourselves to Him in all manly obedience and strenuous good works. —*Religion of the Day*

PRAYER. *O Lord, by meditating on Your inspired Word and by receiving Your Sacraments may I live my life always to please You.*

JULY 10
Value of Self-denial

ONE secret act of self-denial, one sacrifice of inclination to duty, is worth all the mere good thoughts, warm feelings, passionate prayers, in which idle people indulge themselves.

It will give us more comfort on our death-bed to reflect on one deed of self-denying mercy, purity, or humility, than to recollect the shedding of many tears, and much spiritual exultation.

—*Religious Emotion*

PRAYER. *O God, may I show my love for You by performing works of self-denial that please You and not just by works that appeal to me.*

JULY 11
Responding to God's Grace

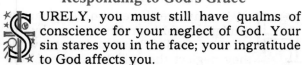

URELY, you must still have qualms of conscience for your neglect of God. Your sin stares you in the face; your ingratitude to God affects you.

Strive to know the Lord, and to secure His favor by *acting* upon these impulses. By them He pleads with you, as well as by your conscience. They are the instruments of His Spirit, stirring you up to seek your true peace.

—*Religious Use of Feelings*

PRAYER. *Lord of all, You continually send me holy inspirations. Help me to respond to them by putting them into practice.*

JULY 12
Believing God's Revelation

ET us but obey God's voice in our hearts, and we shall have no doubts about the truth of Scripture. Find the man who strictly obeys the law within him, and yet is an unbeliever as regards the Bible, and then it will be time enough to consider all that variety of proof by which the truth of the Bible is confirmed to us.

It is bad company or corrupt books which lead to unbelief. It is sin which quenches the Holy Spirit. —*Religious Faith Rational*

PRAYER. *O Lord, You have given us Your revelation through Your inspired Word. Help me to put into practice the Gospel message.*

JULY 13
Obeying Spirit not Letter

HOW many are there who, in a narrow grudging cold-hearted way, go by the letter of God's Commandments, while they neglect the spirit! Instead of considering what Christ wishes them to do, they take His words one by one, and will only accept them in their bare necessary meaning.

They do not throw their hearts upon Scripture and try to consider it as the voice of a Loving Lord speaking to them, but they take it to mean as little as it can.

—Trial of Saul

PRAYER. *Forgive me, my God, for the times I served You in a cold, begrudging way. Please bless me with a generous and loving heart.*

JULY 14
Obedience Is Acceptable to God

BE quite sure that resolute, consistent obedience, though unattended with warm emotion, is far more acceptable to God than all passionate longings to live in His sight.

Learn to live by faith, which is a calm, deliberate, rational principle, full of peace and comfort, and sees Christ and rejoices in Him.

—Religious Use of Feelings

PRAYER. *Almighty God, You have restored to us Your friendship. Enable me to work out my salvation in true obedience to Your will.*

JULY 15
Remembering God's Past Goodness

WE are God's property by creation, by redemption, by regeneration. He has a triple claim upon us.

Let us thankfully commemorate the many mercies He has vouchsafed to us in times past: the many sins He has not remembered, the many dangers He has averted, the many prayers He has answered, the abounding comfort He has from time to time given us.

—Remembrance of Past Mercies

PRAYER. *Merciful Lord, let me always be grateful for Your past favors and responsive to Your grace in the future.*

JULY 16
Mary, the New Eve

IN Mary was to be fulfilled that promise which the world had been looking for during thousands of years. The Seed of the woman, announced to guilty Eve, after long delay was to be born of her. In her, the destinies of the world were to be reversed, and the serpent's head bruised.

On her was bestowed the greatest honor ever put upon anyone of our race. God was taking upon Him her flesh, and humbling Himself to be called her offspring. *—Reverence Due to Mary*

PRAYER. *Dear Jesus, You gave Your Mother to us as You hung dying on the Cross. May she always be my inspiration and model.*

JULY 17
Faith and Action

WHAT, you will ask, are acts of faith? Such as these: to come often to prayer, to kneel down instead of sitting, to behave in God's House otherwise than you would in a common room, to come often to the Holy Sacrament, and to be still and reverent during that sacred service.

These are all acts of faith because they all are acts such as we should perform if we saw and heard Him Who is present, though we see and hear Him not. —*Reverence in God's Presence*

PRAYER. *O Lord, my religious observances give evidence of my faith in You. May my outward conduct be a reflection of my inner devotion.*

JULY 18
Sunday and Holyday Observance

MAY this be our spirit on Sundays and holydays. God rested from His labors on the seventh day, yet He works evermore. Christ entered into His rest, yet He too ever works. We too, while we rest in Christ, should serve Him with steadfast eyes yet active hands.

May we be truly His in our hearts by the recurring celebration of His purifying and holy Feasts. —*Keeping Fast and Festival*

PRAYER. *Blessed Savior, enkindle in my heart a lively devotion to Sunday and holyday observance. Let me share ever more in Your life.*

JULY 19
A Glimpse of Things Divine

THOUGH Moses was not permitted to enter the land of promise, he was vouchsafed a sight of it from a distance. We too, though as yet not admitted to heavenly glory, are given to see much, in preparation for seeing more.

Christ dwells among us in His Church really though invisibly and through its Ordinances fulfills toward us, in a true sense, the promise of the text. —*Reverence in God's Presence*

PRAYER. *Blessed Savior, never let me take for granted the opportunities You give me to encounter You through Your Sacraments.*

JULY 20
Responding to God's Gifts

GOD is in you for righteousness, for sanctification, for redemption, through the Spirit of His Son, and you must use His influences, His operations, not as your own, but as His presence in you.

All your knowledge is from Him; all good thoughts are from Him; all power to pray is from Him; your Baptism is from Him; the consecrated elements are from Him; your growth in holiness is from Him. —*Righteousness*

PRAYER. *Dear Jesus, You continually bestow gifts upon Your followers. Let me always respond to the promptings of Your grace so that I may please You every day of my life.*

107

JULY 21
Following Christ in Penance

PRAYER and fasting have been called the wings of the soul, and they who neither fast nor pray cannot follow Christ. They cannot lift up their hearts.

Great, then, is the contrast between the many and those holy and blessed souls who rise with Christ and set their affection on things above. The one are in light and peace, the others are hurrying along the broad way "which leads to destruction" (Mt 7:13).   —*Rising with Christ*

PRAYER. *Accept the acts of penance I perform, O God, in union with the sacrifice of Christ and let them be an atonement for my sins.*

JULY 22
Showing Gratitude to God

WE may be conscious of the truth of things sacred; we may have no misgivings about the presence of God in church, or about the grace of the Sacraments, and yet we often feel in as ordinary and as unconcerned a mood as if we were altogether unbelievers.

Let us reflect on our callousness after mercies received. May this rouse us to a deeper seriousness, while Christ still continues to intercede for us, and grants us time for repentance!

—*Trial of Saul*

PRAYER. *God of goodness, Your mercy endures forever. Make me always grateful for Your gifts.*

JULY 23
Patience with God

HOW many are there who, when in distress of any kind, forget, like Saul, that their distress, whatever it is, comes from God; that God brings it on them, and that God will remove it in His own way, if they trust in Him.

But who, instead of waiting for His time, take their own way, their own bad way, and impatiently hasten the time, and thus bring on themselves judgment! —*Trial of Saul*

PRAYER. Almighty God, I know there is a time for patience and a time for action. Help me to know when I should wait and seek Your will.

JULY 24
Invisible God Revealed

THIS was one among the benefits of Christ's coming, that the Invisible God was then revealed in the form and history of man.

The Gospels, which contain the memorials of this wonderful grace, are our principal treasures. They may be called the text of the Revelation. The Epistles, especially St. Paul's, are as comments upon it, unfolding and illustrating it and thus everywhere dutifully preaching His Person, work, and will. —*Saving Knowledge*

PRAYER. Dear Lord Jesus, You emptied Yourself of the glory that is Yours as God and became man. Let me encounter the Father through You.

JULY 25
Obedience Follows Belief

S T. John says, "Hereby do we know that we know Him, if we keep His commandments" (1 Jn 2:3). Thus the whole duty and work of a Christian is made up of these two parts, Faith and Obedience: "looking unto Jesus," the Divine Object as well as Author of our faith, and acting according to His will.

A certain frame of mind, certain notions, affections, and tempers, a necessary condition of a saving state, will follow if our hearts grow into these two chief objects. —*Saving Knowledge*

PRAYER. *O God, help me to know and love You more and to rejoice in Your Commandments.*

JULY 26
Conforming to the Gospel

H OW then is it possible that a man can duly examine his feelings and affections by the light within him? How can he accurately decide upon their character, whether Christian or not?

It is necessary that he go out of himself to ascertain the nature of the principles which govern him; he must have recourse to his works, and compare them with Scripture, as the only evidence whether or not his heart is perfect with God. —*Saving Knowledge*

PRAYER. *Christ, my Savior, let my life always conform to Your teaching. Let the Sacred Scriptures and Your Church ever be my guide.*

JULY 27
Living in Christ's Presence

T O know God and Christ, in Scripture language, seems to mean to live under the conviction of His presence, Who is to our bodily eyes unseen. It is, in fact, to have faith, according to St. Paul's account of faith, as the substance and evidence of what is invisible.

It is Gospel faith; for only in the Gospel has God so revealed Himself, as to allow of that kind of faith which may be called, in a special manner, knowledge. —*Saving Knowledge*

PRAYER. *Grant, O Lord, that I may always feel Your presence within me wherever I go. And may I always act accordingly.*

JULY 28
All on Trial

W E are all on our trial. Every one who lives is on his trial, whether he will serve God or not.

Many other trials besides Adam's are recorded in Scripture, for our warning and instruction; that we may be reminded that we too are on trial, that we may be encouraged by the examples of those who have stood their trial well and not fallen, and may be sobered and put on our guard by the instances of others who have fallen under their trial. —*Trial of Saul*

PRAYER. *Come, Holy Spirit, and strengthen me to imitate the Apostles, Martyrs, and all the Saints who persevered in their time of trial.*

JULY 29
God Chooses the Lowly

GOD chose David whose occupation was that of a shepherd, for He chooses not the great men of the world. He passes by the rich and noble; He chooses "the poor, rich in faith and heirs of the Kingdom" (Jas 2:5).

The Angel appeared to the shepherds as they kept watch over their sheep at night. The most solitary, the most unlearned, God hears, God looks upon, God visits, God blesses, God brings to glory, if he is but "rich in faith." —*Call of David*

PRAYER. *Dear Jesus, help me to be rich in faith, so that I may be chosen by You and brought to Your Kingdom.*

JULY 30
Our Hope in Christ

SURELY, even our best doings have that taint of sinfulness pervading them, which will remind us ever where our True Hope is lodged.

Men are satisfied with themselves, not when they attempt but when they neglect the details of duty. Disobedience blinds the conscience; obedience makes it keen-sighted and sensitive. The more we do, the more shall we trust in Christ. —*Saving Knowledge*

PRAYER. *Divine Savior, I rely on Your infinite goodness and promises. Help me to live according to Your will and attain eternal life.*

JULY 31
To Walk in the Ordinances of God

AS far as a man has reason to hope that he is *consistent,* so far may he humbly trust that he has true faith. To be consistent, to "walk in all the ordinances of the Lord blameless" (Ps 119:1), is his one business; still, all along looking reverently toward the Great Object of faith, the Father, the Son, and the Holy Spirit, Three Persons, One God.

Certainly he will have enough to direct his course by, with God in his eye, and his work in his hand.
                                              —*Saving Knowledge*

PRAYER. *Graciously accept, dear Lord, my good intentions and ever let me be a faithful follower of Your divine commands.*

AUGUST 1
Difficulties in This World

LOOK upon the world in this light—its sights of sorrows are to calm you, and its pleasant sights to try you.

Make up your mind to the prospect of sustaining a certain measure of pain and trouble in your passage through life; by the blessing of God this will prepare you for it—it will make you thoughtful and resigned without interfering with your cheerfulness.

                                              —*Scripture a Record*

PRAYER. *Everlasting Lord, help me to see that the difficulties of this life are merely Your way of bringing me closer to You.*

AUGUST 2
Blessed Hope in God's Promises

LET us rejoice now, not as if we have attained but in hope of attaining. Let us take our present happiness not as our true rest but as a type and shadow of it.

If we now enjoy God's ordinances, let us not cease to pray that they may prepare us for His presence hereafter. If we enjoy the presence of friends, let them remind us of the Communion of Saints before His throne. Let us draw hope from everything. —*Season of Epiphany*

PRAYER. *Relying on Your infinite goodness and Your promises, O God, I firmly hope to be with You in Your Kingdom.*

AUGUST 3
God Does Not Abandon Sinners

IF God seems to be making us His instruments for any purpose of His, this will create in us the belief that He has not utterly forsaken us in spite of our sins.

If, for all our infirmities, we can point to some occasions on which we have sacrificed anything for God's service, or to any work which we have accomplished to God's honor and glory, this may fill us with the humble hope that God is working in us and is at peace with us. —*Sins of Infirmity*

PRAYER. *Heavenly Father, accept the small sacrifices I make to atone for my sins in union with those of Christ my Savior.*

AUGUST 4
God's Plan for Us

THE world is blind, and God hides His providence. Whether Christ is at our doors or not, but a few may have grace enough to conjecture; but that He is calling upon us to prepare for His coming is evident to those who have religious eyes and ears.

Let us recollect how mysteriously little things are in this world connected with great; how single moments, improved or wasted, are the salvation or ruin of all-important interests.

—Secrecy of Divine Visitations

PRAYER. *O God, I know that Your providence always looks after me and nothing in my life is hidden from You. Be my guide and guardian.*

AUGUST 5
Vocations to the Religious Life

MAY the good Lord save His Church in this her hour of peril; when Satan seeks to sap and corrupt where he dare not openly assault!

May He raise up instruments of His grace, not ignorant of the devices of the Evil One, with seeing eyes, and strong hearts, and vigorous arms to defend the treasure of the Faith and to arouse and alarm their slumbering brethren!

—Secrecy of Divine Visitations

PRAYER. *Jesus, my Lord, inspire young men and women to take up the challenge You are offering them in the religious life.*

AUGUST 6
Treasure of the Blessed Sacrament

WHEN Christ ascended into the Mount, "His face did shine as the sun" (Mt 17:2). Such is the glorious presence which faith sees in Holy Communion, though everything looks as usual to the natural man.

Not the light of the sun sevenfold is so awfully bright—if we could see as the Angels do—as that seed of eternal life, which by eating and drinking we lay up in our hearts against the day of His coming. —*State of Grace*

PRAYER. *Dearest Savior, You have given Your Body and Blood to me as spiritual food and drink. Let me ever be grateful!*

AUGUST 7
Repentance

THERE are such imperfections, such inconsistencies in the heart and life of even the better sort of men that continual repentance must ever go hand in hand with our endeavors to obey.

Much we need the grace of Christ's Blood to wash us from the guilt we daily incur; much need we the aid of His promised Spirit! And surely He will grant all the riches of His mercy to His true servants. —*Test of Religious Earnestness*

PRAYER. *Grant me, Almighty God, an awareness of my sinfulness so that, moved by Your grace, I may turn to You for forgiveness.*

AUGUST 8
God Provides Direction

FALSE wisdom, of which St. Paul speaks, is trusting our own powers for arriving at religious truth, instead of taking what is divinely provided for us, whether in nature or in revelation. This is the way of the world.

In the world, Reason is set against Conscience, and usurps its power; and hence men become "wise in their own conceits" (Rom 11:25) and, leaning to their own understandings, "err from the truth" (Jas 5:19).   —*Self-wise Inquirer*

PRAYER. *Purify my heart, dear God, through the light of Your revelation and the guidance of Your Church.*

AUGUST 9
Diligence in Serving God

YOU say, "How can I pray to see Christ, who am so unclean?" Do you expect in this life ever to be clean? Yes, in one sense, by the presence of the Holy Spirit within you.

But if by "clean" you mean free from that infection of nature, the least drop of which is sufficient to dishonor all your services, clean you never will be till you have paid the debt of sin. What Christ asks of you is not sinlessness, but diligence.   —*Shrinking from Christ's Coming*

PRAYER. *Blessed Savior, help me to persevere in my service to You. Through the presence of the Holy Spirit in my soul, strengthen me.*

AUGUST 10
God's Prompting by Grace

WHILE God remains in the highest heaven, He comes to judge the world—and while He judges the world, He is in us also, bearing us up. God the Son is without, but God the Spirit is within.

That Spirit is vouchsafed to us here; and if we yield ourselves to His gracious influences, so that He draws up our thoughts and wills to heavenly things, and becomes one with us, He will assuredly be still in us and give us confidence at the Day of Judgment.—*Shrinking from Christ's Coming*

PRAYER. *Holy Spirit of God, be with me each day of my life so that I may always serve You in every thought, word, and action.*

AUGUST 11
Living in God's Presence

DO you habitually unlock your hearts and subject your thoughts to Almighty God? Are you living in this conviction of His Presence and have you this special witness that His Presence is really set up within you unto your salvation, that you live in the sense of it?

Do you believe and act on the belief, that His light shines through your heart, as the sun's beams through a room? —*Sincerity and Hypocrisy*

PRAYER. *Ever-present God, let me reflect Your grace and goodness wherever I go.*

AUGUST 12
Proof of Our Love

A MAN says to himself, "How am I to know I am in earnest?" I would suggest to him: Make some sacrifice, do some distasteful thing, which you are not actually obliged to do.

Bring home to your mind that in fact you do love your Savior, that you do hate sin, that you have put aside the present world. Thus you will have evidence (to a certain point) that you are not using mere words. —*Test of Religious Earnestness*

PRAYER. *Almighty God, grant me the grace to give me courage to witness to You wherever I go.*

AUGUST 13
Renewal of the Lord's Death

T AKE this view of the Lord's Supper as the appointed means of obtaining the great blessings you need. The daily prayers of the Christian do but spring from, and are referred back to, his attendance on it.

Christ died once: by communicating in His Sacrament, you renew the Lord's death; you bring into the midst of you that Sacrifice which took away the sins of the world; you appropriate the benefit of it, while you eat it under the species of bread and wine. —*Sins of Ignorance*

PRAYER. *Eucharistic Lord, come into my heart and rule over my whole life. Grant that I may ever live in You, and You in me.*

AUGUST 14
Self-knowledge

LET us approach God, confessing that we do not know ourselves; that we are more guilty than we can possibly understand, and can but timidly hope, not confidently determine, that we have true faith.

Let us take comfort in our being still in a state of grace, though we have no certain pledge of salvation. Let us beg Him to enlighten us, and comfort us; to forgive us all our sins, teaching us those we do not see and enabling us to overcome them. —*Sins of Ignorance*

PRAYER. *Lord, help me to know myself and to know You; to die to self and live in You.*

AUGUST 15
Mary's Gifts of Grace

WHO can estimate the holiness and perfection of her who was chosen to be the Mother of Christ? What must have been the transcendent purity of her whom the Creator Spirit condescended to overshadow with His miraculous presence?

What must have been her gifts who was chosen to be the only near earthly relative of the Son of God, the only one whom He was bound by nature to revere and look up to, the one appointed to train and instruct Him? —*Reverence Due to Mary*

PRAYER. *Blessed Jesus, when You hung on the Cross, You gave us Your holy Mother. May she always keep me in her tender care.*

AUGUST 16
Apostolicity of the Church

CHRISTIANITY has spread from a center by regularly formed bodies, descendants of the three thousand, who, after St. Peter's preaching on the day of Pentecost, joined themselves to the Apostles' doctrine and fellowship.

We know that the ministers of the Church are descended from the Apostles. Amid all the changes of this world, the Church built upon St. Peter and the rest has continued until now in the unbroken line of the ministry. —*Unity of the Church*

PRAYER. *Almighty God, thank You for making me a member of the One, Holy, Catholic, and Apostolic Church led by the Pope, the Vicar of Christ.*

AUGUST 17
Christ, Living Son of the Father

IT is impossible for a Christian to meditate on the Gospels without feeling beyond all manner of doubt that He Who is the subject of them is God. But it is very possible to speak in a vague way of His love toward us.

It is very possible to use the name of Christ, yet not at all to realize that He is the Living Son of the Father or to have any anchor for our faith within us so as to be fortified against the risk of future defection. —*Tears of Christ*

PRAYER. *O God, Your Son emptied Himself and took a human form for the salvation of the world. Help me to acknowledge His divinity.*

AUGUST 18
Pray for Knowledge of Our Duty

WAIT diligently on God, pray Him earnestly to teach us more of our duty and to impress the love of it on our hearts.

Pray Him to enable us to obey both in that free spirit, which can act right without reasoning and calculation, and yet with the caution of those who know their salvation depends on obedience in little things, from love of the truth as manifested in Him, Who is the Living Truth come upon earth, "the Way, the Truth, and the Life" (Jn 14:6). —*Spiritual Mind*

PRAYER. *O Lord, grant me a greater awareness of my duties toward You and my neighbor. Enable me to carry them out as best I can.*

AUGUST 19
Walking through Life with Christ

CHRISTIANS, on looking back on years past, will feel, at least in a degree, that Christ has been with them, though they knew it not, only believed it, at the time.

They will savor immortality rising upon their minds, as if in token that God has been with them, and investing all that has taken place— which before seemed to them but earthly—with glory. —*Spiritual Presence of Christ*

PRAYER. *My faith, O Jesus, gives me confidence in Your presence and assistance in time of trouble. Comfort me when I am in distress.*

AUGUST 20
Deliberate Sin

THE Christian is a soldier. He may have many falls. These need not hinder his joy in the Gospel. He must be humbled indeed but not downcast.

But willful sin in any shape proves that he is not an honest soldier of Christ. If it is habitual and deliberate, of course it destroys his hope. But if it be less than deliberate and yet of the nature of willful sin, it is sufficient, though not to separate him at once from Christ, yet to separate him from the inward vision of Him. —*State of Grace*

PRAYER. *Blessed Savior, let me ever be conscious of even my small sins because they are an offense to You, and grant me sincere repentance.*

AUGUST 21
Peace of Soul amid Imperfections

NO one on earth is free from imperfection and sin, no one but has much continually to repent of. St. Paul bids us "rejoice in the Lord always" (Phil 4:4). He describes Christians as having peace with God and rejoicing in hope of His glory.

Sins of infirmity then, such as arise from the infection of our original nature and not from deliberation and willfulness, have no divine warrant to keep us from joy and peace.—*State of Grace*

PRAYER. *Holy Spirit of God, inspire me by Your grace so that I may avoid not only serious sin but also those small sins that keep me from perfection.*

123

AUGUST 22
Zeal in Doing God's Will

ZEAL is one of the elementary religious qualifications; that is, one of those which are essential in the very notion of a religious man. A man cannot be said to be in earnest in religion, till he magnifies his God and Savior.

In a word, a religious temper is one of loyalty toward God. It is the main principle in *all* religious service to love God above all things. Zeal is to love Him above all men, above our dearest and most intimate friends. —*Christian Zeal*

PRAYER. *God of goodness, stir up in my heart the ardent desire always to do Your will and to love You above all things.*

AUGUST 23
Characteristics of Christian Life

LET us learn from whatever gifts of mind we have henceforth to keep them under and to subject them to innocence, simplicity, and truth. Let our characters be formed upon faith, love, contemplativeness, modesty, meekness, humility.

Let the tumult of error teach us the simplicity of truth; the miseries of guilt, the peace of innocence; and the many inventions of the reason, the stability of faith. —*State of Innocence*

PRAYER. *Blessed Savior, let every day of my life be a sincere attempt to put into practice the simple virtues that mark Your followers.*

AUGUST 24
In God's Own Time

HOUGH David received the gift of God's Holy Spirit, yet nothing came of it all at once. He still seemed like any other man.

So it is with Christian Baptism. Nothing shows for some time that the Spirit of God is come into the child. Sooner or later that work of God is manifested, which was at first secret. God is with those whom He has chosen, and in His own time and way He fashions His Saints for His everlasting Kingdom. —*Call of David*

PRAYER. *Dear Lord, You work in mysterious ways. Let Your light shine upon me, and in Your own good time and way lead me to Your Kingdom.*

AUGUST 25
Forgotten and Unconfessed Sins

MOST dreadful thought, if an account lies against us in God's books, which we have never manfully encountered, never inquired into, never even prayed against, only and simply *forgotten*.

May God give us all grace ever to pray Him to show us how to unburden ourselves—how to secure to ourselves again those gifts which, for what we know, we have forfeited. —*State of Salvation*

PRAYER. *Blessed Savior, if I have deliberately neglected to confess something serious, allow me the grace of sorrow and repentance.*

AUGUST 26
Seeking Happiness Correctly

LEFT to ourselves, we seek good from the world, but cannot find it; in youth we look forward, and in age we look back. Seek we great things? We must seek them where they really are to be found, and in the way in which they are to be found.

We must seek them as He has set them before us, Who came into the world to enable us to gain them. We must be willing to give up present hope for future enjoyment, this world for the unseen.

—Jeremiah a Lesson

PRAYER. *Blessed Savior, You told us that where our treasure is, there will be our heart. You are my treasure! May I seek You and You alone.*

AUGUST 27
Newborn Creatures in Christ

THE Gospel covenant is the means of introducing us into a state of life so different from that in which we were born that it may be called a new creation.

As that which is created differs from what is not yet created, so the Christian differs from the natural man. He is brought into a new world and, as being in that new world, is invested with powers and privileges which he absolutely had not in the way of nature.

—State of Salvation

PRAYER. *O God, You have given me rebirth through the Sacrament of Baptism. May my life always reflect Your divine work in me.*

AUGUST 28
Refreshing Our Spirit in God

WE do not know perhaps, what or where our pain is; we are so used to it that we do not call it pain. Still so it is; we need a relief to our hearts that they may be dark and sullen no longer, or that they may not go on feeding upon themselves.

We need to escape from ourselves to something beyond. And much as we may wish it otherwise and may try to make idols to ourselves, nothing short of God's presence is our true refuge!

—*Thought of God*

PRAYER. *In times of trouble, be a source of solace for me, O God. Let me acknowledge that in You I will find peace and contentment.*

AUGUST 29
Turning the Other Cheek

DO not be too eager to suppose you are ill-treated for your religion's sake. Make as light of matters as you can. And beware of being severe on those who lead careless lives, or whom you think or know to be ill-treating you.

Do not dwell on such matters. Turn your mind away from them. Avoid all gloominess. Be kind and gentle to those who are perverse, and you will very often, please God, gain them over.

—*Endurance of Censure*

PRAYER. *Long-suffering God, help me to have patience with others and with myself at all times.*

AUGUST 30
Letting Our Light Shine

WE must manifest the Kingdom of heaven upon earth. The light of divine truth must proceed *from* our hearts and shine out *upon* everything we are and everything we do.

They who are holy in spirit are holy in body. They who submit their wills to Christ bow their bodies. They who offer the heart bow the knee. They who have faith in His Name bow the head. They who honor His Cross inwardly are not ashamed of it before men.

—*Offerings for the Sanctuary*

PRAYER. *Dear Jesus, You want Christians to let their light shine before the world. Help me to be an example to all with whom I come in contact.*

AUGUST 31
Persistence in Prayer

THEY who pray for the Spirit's saving help do not all at once gain what they seek. But if they come continually day by day, if they come determined to go on seeking Him, trusting Him, such men *will* gain it.

They will find, even while still seeking; He will answer them, and they will find themselves saved wondrously, when their crown seemed at a distance. —*Strictness of Law of Christ*

PRAYER. *Dear Jesus, You emphasized the need for perseverance in prayer. Let me understand that what I ask for might be slow in coming.*

SEPTEMBER 1
Meeting Christ in Our Work

A DILIGENT Christian will feel that the true contemplation of the Savior lies *in* his worldly business; that as Christ is seen in the poor, and in the persecuted, and in children, so is He seen in the employments which He puts upon His chosen.

He will see Christ revealed to his soul amid the ordinary actions of the day, as by a sort of Sacrament. Thus he will take his worldly business as a gift from Him, and will love it as such.

—*Doing Glory to God*

PRAYER. *Heavenly Father, You have given me talents to use for Your glory. Help me to offer my work to You each day.*

SEPTEMBER 2
Effects of Private Prayer

LET your morning and evening thoughts be points of rest for your mind's eye, and let those thoughts be upon the narrow way, and the blessedness of heaven.

Men in general will know nothing of this; they witness not your private prayers. But your friends will gain comfort from your example; they will see your good works, and trace them to their true source, the influences of the Holy Spirit sought and obtained by prayer. —*Times of Private Prayer*

PRAYER. *Sanctify me, O God, so that I do not simply mouth words in my prayers. Let them be a genuine means of communicating with You.*

SEPTEMBER 3
God's Precious Gifts

IF we are in possession of precious things, let us rather devote them to God than keep them for ourselves. And let us never forget that all we can give, though of His creation, is worthless in comparison with the more precious gifts which He bestows on us in the Gospel.

Though our Font and Altar were of costly marble, though our communion vessels were of gold and jewels, what is all this compared to Christ, the Son of God and Son of Man, present here, but unseen! *—Offerings for the Sanctuary*

PRAYER. *O God, let me always be grateful for what You have given me. May I especially treasure the great Sacrament of Christ's presence.*

SEPTEMBER 4
Sufficient Grace

LET us beg of Christ an increase of faith, a more lively perception of the curse under which the world lies, and of our own personal demerits.

Let us beg a more understanding view of the mystery of His Cross, a more devout reliance on the virtue of it, and a more confident persuasion that He will never put upon us more than we can bear, never afflict His brethren with any woe except for their own highest benefit.

—Tears of Christ

PRAYER. *In times of trial, dear Lord, let me always believe that Your grace is sufficient for me.*

130

SEPTEMBER 5
Willingness To Change

E are by nature what we are, very sinful and corrupt, we know. However, we like to be what we are and for many reasons it is very unpleasant to us to change.

We cannot change ourselves. This too we know full well, or, at least, a very little experience will teach us. God alone can change us. What then is it that we who profess religion lack? This—a willingness to *be* changed, a willingness to allow Almighty God to change us.

—*Testimony of Conscience*

PRAYER. *Almighty God, let me ever be willing to allow You to change me as You will.*

SEPTEMBER 6
God's Presence in Prayer

T stated times, when we gather up our thoughts to pray, and draw out our petitions in an orderly and clear manner, the act of faith is likely to be stronger and more earnest.

Then we realize more perfectly the presence of that God Whom we do not see, Who bore the weight of our infirmities once for all, that in all our troubles we might seek Him, and find grace in time of need. —*Times of Private Prayer*

PRAYER. *Almighty God, cleanse my heart and make it fertile to be a source of holiness for me and of good example to my neighbor.*

131

SEPTEMBER 7
Christ Sanctifies Labor

WHEREAS Adam was sentenced to labor as a punishment, Christ has by His coming sanctified it as a means of grace and a sacrifice of thanksgiving, a sacrifice cheerfully to be offered up to the Father in His name.

It is very easy to speak and teach this, difficult to do it; to use this world as not abusing it, to be active and diligent in this world's affairs, yet not for this world's sake, but for God's sake. —*Doing Glory to God*

PRAYER. *Father of lights, enable me to radiate Your light to others in my daily work.*

SEPTEMBER 8
Quiet Holiness

OBSERVE the lesson which we gain from the history of the Blessed Virgin; that the highest graces of the soul may be matured in private, and without those fierce trials to which many are exposed.

God gives His Holy Spirit to us silently; and the silent duties of every day are blest to the sufficient sanctification of thousands, whom the world knows not. The Blessed Virgin is a memorial of this; and it is consoling as well as instructive to know it. —*Reverence Due to Mary*

PRAYER. *Lord Jesus, Your Blessed Mother spent her life in quiet service to You. Let me realize that You see my private unknown service.*

132

SEPTEMBER 9
Pride and Lack of Reverence

THOUGH grave and solemn, the Pharisee was not reverent; he spoke in a haughty, proud way, and made a long sentence, thanking God that he was not as other men are, and despising the Publican.

But the Publican behaved very differently. Observe how he came to worship God; "he stood afar off; he lifted not up so much as his eyes unto heaven, but beat upon his breast, saying, 'God be merciful to me a sinner' " (Lk 18:13).

—Reverence in Worship

PRAYER. *O Jesus, You extolled humility and warned against pride. Help me to imitate the humility of the Publican.*

SEPTEMBER 10
Fellow Citizens with the Saints

LET us endeavor to become friends of God and fellow citizens with the Saints. Not by sinless purity, for we have it not. Not in our deeds, for we have none to show. Not in our Baptism, for it is outward.

But in that which is the fruit of Baptism within us. Not a word but a power, not a name but a reality—an honest purpose, an unreserved, entire submission of ourselves to our Maker, Redeemer, and Judge.

—Testimony of Conscience

PRAYER. *O God, let me always call on the grace given to me in Baptism to live a life pleasing to You. Help me to be a fellow citizen with the Saints.*

133

SEPTEMBER 11
Obedience the True Test

"I F you love Me, keep My Commandments" (Jn 14:15). This is all that is put upon us—difficult indeed to perform but easy to understand because Christ has done everything else.

He has freely chosen us, died for us, regenerated us, and now ever lives for us. What remains? Simply that we should do as He has done to us showing forth His glory by good works. Thus an orthodox faith and an obedient life is the whole duty of man. —*Saving Knowledge*

PRAYER. *My faith, O my Savior, leads me to obey Your divine Commandments. With the help of Your grace, I will do my best to please You.*

SEPTEMBER 12
Saving Effects of Christ's Sacrifice

COME to God day by day, entreating Him for all the sins of your whole life. This is the way to keep your baptismal robe bright.

Let it be washed as your garments of this world are, again and again; washed in the most holy, most precious, of all streams, Christ's Blood, Who is without blemish and without spot. It is thus that the Church of God, each individual member of it, becomes all glorious within, and filled with grace. —*Transgressions and Infirmities*

PRAYER. *By Your Death on the Cross, Blessed Savior, You have cleansed me of my sins. Make me always appreciate Your saving sacrifice.*

SEPTEMBER 13
Seek God's Forgiveness Promptly

NEVER suffer sin to remain upon you. Let it not grow old in you. Wipe it off while it is fresh, else it will stain. Let it not get ingrained.

Beware of suffering sin in yourselves if for no other reason than this, you will forget you have committed it and never repent of it at all. Repent of it while you know it. Let it not be wiped from your memory without being first wiped away from your soul. —*Transgressions and Infirmities*

PRAYER. *Most merciful Father, do not let me remain in sin. Help me to repent quickly and to ask forgiveness through Jesus my Redeemer.*

SEPTEMBER 14
We Glory in the Cross of Jesus

AS we gain happiness through suffering, so do we arrive at holiness through infirmity, because man's very condition is a fallen one. In passing out of the country of sin, he necessarily passes through it.

Hence it is that holy men are kept from regarding themselves with satisfaction, or resting in anything short of our Lord's death, as their ground of confidence. For, though that death has already wrought life in them, yet to themselves they seem but sinners. —*Sins of Infirmity*

PRAYER. *We adore You, O Christ, and we bless You, because by Your holy Cross You have redeemed the world.*

SEPTEMBER 15
Truth and Grace

HE Prophet Isaiah (33:17) tells us that under the Gospel covenant God's servants will have the privilege of seeing those heavenly sights which were but shadowed out in the Law. Before Christ came was the time of shadows.

When He came, He brought truth as well as grace. As He Who is the Truth has come to us, so does He in return require that we should be true in our dealings with Him. —*Unreal Words*

PRAYER. *Eternal Father, thank You for the wonders You sent us in Jesus. Grant that I may seek You fervently and serve You sincerely.*

SEPTEMBER 16
Knowing Oneself

ET us guard against frivolity, love of display, love of being talked about, love of seeming original. Let us aim at meaning what we say, and saying what we mean. Let us aim at knowing when we understand a truth and when we do not. When we do not, let us take it on faith and let us profess to do so.

Let us receive the truth in reverence and pray God to give us a good will, and divine light, and spiritual strength that it may bear fruit within us. —*Unreal Words*

PRAYER. *Almighty God, help me to know and be myself. Never let me be led by vanity to pretend to know more or to be more than I am.*

SEPTEMBER 17
Celebrating the Holydays

HOLYDAYS are not duly observed. Our Church abridged the number of Holydays, thinking it right to have but a few; but we account any as too much.

It would be a powerful evidence of our earnestness if we testified for Christ at some inconvenience to ourselves; if all who loved the Lord Jesus Christ in sincerity made it a practice to throng the churches on the weekday Festivals and various Holy Seasons. —*Use of Saints' Days*

PRAYER. *Heavenly Father, do not let me regard the Holydays of Your Church as inconveniences. Help me to celebrate them by participating at Mass and Communion.*

SEPTEMBER 18
Unity of the Church

CHRISTIANS should live together in a visible society here on earth, not as an unconnected multitude, but united one with another, by an established order, so as to appear and to act as one. And this *is* a doctrine neglected far and wide.

What possible way is there of many men acting together, except by forming themselves into a visible body or society, regulated by certain laws and officers? —*Unity of the Church*

PRAYER. *Blessed Savior, at the Last Supper You prayed for the unity of Your followers. Bring all Christians closer while awaiting true unity.*

SEPTEMBER 19
Seeing as God Sees

THERE are ten thousand ways of looking at this world but only one right way. It is the way in which God looks at the world.

Aim at seeing things as God sees them. Aim at forming judgments such as God forms. Aim at looking at the life to come and the world unseen as God does. All things that we see are but shadows to us and delusions, unless we enter into what they really mean. —*Unreal Words*

PRAYER. Most merciful Father, I know that my limited knowledge does not always give me a proper perspective. Assist me to view the world as You see it.

SEPTEMBER 20
How To View Suffering

LET us not forget, that, as we are called to be Saints, so we are, by that very calling, called to suffer; and if we suffer, we must not think it strange concerning the fiery trial that is to try us.

We should not be puffed up by our privilege of suffering, nor bring suffering needlessly upon us, nor be eager to make out we have suffered for Christ, when we have but suffered for our faults, or not at all. —*Use of Saints' Days*

PRAYER. Your Saints, O Jesus, were called upon to suffer for their faith. Unite my sufferings to Yours and help me to carry my cross with resignation.

138

SEPTEMBER 21
End Does Not Justify Means

HOW many are there who, when in unpleasant situations, are tempted to do what is wrong in order to get out of them.

They have, perhaps, unkind parents, and they are so uncomfortable at home that they take the first opportunity which presents itself of getting away. They marry irreligious persons, merely from impatience to get out of their present discomfort. They forget that God can take it away in His good time, and without their sin.—*Trial of Saul*

PRAYER. *When I am tempted to "cut corners" and not "go by the book," dear Jesus, lead me back to the right path.*

SEPTEMBER 22
Idle Curiosity Leads to Disobedience

CURIOSITY strangely moves us to disobedience, in order that we may have experience of the pleasure of disobedience.

And we thus intrude into things forbidden in various ways; in reading what we should not read, in hearing what we should not hear, in seeing what we should not see, in going into company whither we should not go, in acting as if we were our own masters where we should obey. —*Curiosity a Temptation*

PRAYER. *Father in heaven, help me to cultivate a holy curiosity—one that fosters obedience to Your law and Your will.*

SEPTEMBER 23
Looking Forward to Retirement

SOME look to their last years as a time of retirement, in which they may *both* enjoy themselves *and* prepare for heaven.

If they are at present *not* serving God, when at length they *do* put aside worldly cares and turn to God, that time must necessarily be a time of deep humiliation if it is to be acceptable to Him, not a comfortable retirement. Who ever heard of a pleasurable, easy, joyous repentance.
—*Doing Glory to God*

PRAYER. *Merciful God, help me to serve You diligently throughout my life, so that my retirement will be a time of giving even greater service to You.*

SEPTEMBER 24
God's Revelation Our Guide

THE Gospel has come to us not merely to make us good subjects, good citizens, good members of society, but to make us members of the New Jerusalem and "fellow citizens with the Saints and of the household of God" (Eph 2:19).

If one is not aiming at something beyond the power of the natural man, he is not really a Christian, or one of the elect. The Gospel offers to us things supernatural.
—*Visible Church*

PRAYER. *Lord Jesus, You gave us the Gospel and the Church as our guardian through life. Let me not deviate from their guidance.*

SEPTEMBER 25
True Children of the Church

GOD grant to us a simple, reverent, affectionate, temper that we may truly be the Church's children and fit subjects of her instructions! This gained, the rest through His grace will follow.

This is the temper of those "little ones," whose Angels "do always behold the face" (Mt 18:10) of our heavenly Father; of those for whom Apostles endured all things, and whom Christ "nourishes and cherishes" (Eph 5:29) even as His own flesh. —*Visible Church*

PRAYER. *Heavenly Father, teach me to cultivate the childlike qualities of soul that mark the followers of Christ. Let me be a true child of God.*

SEPTEMBER 26
Christ's Mystical Body

CHRIST has made Himself a Temple not out of inanimate things but of men. Not gold and silver, jewels and fine linen, and skill of man to use them, make the House of God, but worshipers—the souls and bodies of men whom He has redeemed.

He claims us as His own, not one by one, but altogether, as one great company. All of us, and every one, and every part of every one, make up His Mystical Body. —*Visible Church*

PRAYER. *I became Your temple, O Blessed Trinity, and a member of Christ's Mystical Body when I was baptized. May I always be aware of this.*

SEPTEMBER 27
Christ—the Great High Priest

WHEN Christ had come, suffered, and ascended, He was henceforth ever near us. He is the only Ruler and Priest in His Church.

Christ's priests have no priesthood but His. They are merely His shadows and organs; they are His outward signs. What they do, He does. When they baptize, He is baptizing. When they bless, He is blessing. He is in all acts of His Church, and all are His.

—*Waiting for Christ*

PRAYER. *Bless, O Lord, those in Your Church who share in Your priesthood. Help them to sanctify Your people.*

SEPTEMBER 28
Glory of Christians

ALL Christians are kings in God's sight; they are kings in His unseen Kingdom, in His spiritual world, in the Communion of Saints. They seem like other men, but they have crowns on their heads, and glorious robes around them, and Angels to wait on them, though our bodily eyes see it not.

Such are all Christians, high and low; all Christians who remain in that state in which Holy Baptism placed them. —*Call of David*

PRAYER. *Heavenly Father, bless me with spiritual eyes so that I may see what a great privilege it is to be a Christian.*

SEPTEMBER 29
Our Heavenly Home

I N the unseen world where Christ has entered, all is peace. There is no more death, nor any more sin, nor any more guilt; no more penitence; no more trial; no infirmity to depress us; but only the light of God's countenance.

That is our *home*. Here we are but on pilgrimage, and Christ is calling us home. He calls us to His many mansions, which He has prepared.

—Warfare Condition of Victory

PRAYER. *Blessed Jesus, You told Your followers that You would go before them to prepare a place for them. May I be among those admitted to Your Kingdom.*

SEPTEMBER 30
Appreciating the Redemption

H E watches for Christ who is zealous in seeking and honoring Him. He looks out for Him in all that happens and would not be surprised if he found that He was coming at once.

And he watches *with* Christ, who does not forget what He has suffered for him. He watches with Christ whoever commemorates and renews in his own person Christ's Cross and Agony.

—Watching

PRAYER. *Dear Jesus, help me always be mindful of what You have done for my salvation. Let me appreciate Your great love for me.*

OCTOBER 1
Judge Not

ALL of us are in danger of hastily finding fault with others; not considering that unless we have faithfully obeyed our conscience, we are no fit judges of them at all.

It is only as we labor to change our nature, through God's help, that we begin to discern the beauty of holiness. Then, we find reason to suspect our own judgments of what is truly good and perceive our own blindness.   —*Truth Hidden*

PRAYER. *God of goodness, help me to avoid judging others. Teach me to accept all persons for what they are—Your children.*

OCTOBER 2
The Angels of God

WE are not told in Scripture about the Angels for nothing, but for practical purposes; nor can I conceive a use of our knowledge more practical than to make it connect the sight of this world with the thought of another.

It is a great comfort to reflect that, wherever we go, we have those about us who are ministering to us, though we see them not. If we attain to heaven, we shall become the companions of the blessed Angels!   —*Powers of Nature*

PRAYER. *Almighty God, on many occasions You have revealed Your Angels to humankind. May I one day join them in Your eternal presence.*

OCTOBER 3
The Honor Due Angels

HERE have been ages of the world in which men have thought too much of Angels and paid them excessive honor, honored them so perversely as to forget the supreme worship due to Almighty God.

But the sin of what is called an educated age is just the reverse: to account slightly of them, or not at all, resting in things seen and forgetting unseen things and our ignorance about them. *—Powers of Nature*

PRAYER. *Angel of God, my guardian dear, to whom God's love commits me here, ever this day be at my side, to light and guard, to rule and guide.*

OCTOBER 4
Our Spiritual Powers

F we are true to ourselves, nothing can really thwart us. Our warfare is not with carnal weapons but with heavenly. The world does not understand what our real power is and where it lies.

Until we put ourselves into its hands of our own act, it can do nothing against us. Till we leave off patience, meekness, purity, resignation, and peace, it can do nothing against that Cause which is ours, as it has been the Cause of all Saints before us. *—Weapons of Saints*

PRAYER. *Dear Jesus, help me to overcome the powers of evil by cultivating the virtues of the Gospel. Let me witness to You wherever I go.*

145

OCTOBER 5
Witnesses of Christ

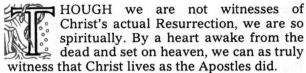

THOUGH we are not witnesses of Christ's actual Resurrection, we are so spiritually. By a heart awake from the dead and set on heaven, we can as truly witness that Christ lives as the Apostles did.

He that believes in the Son of God has the witness in himself. Truth bears witness by itself to its Divine Author. He who obeys God conscientiously, and lives holily, forces all about him to believe and tremble before the unseen power of Christ. —*Witnesses of the Resurrection*

PRAYER. Accept, O Lord, the service of my life so that I may pass to heavenly glory by witnessing to You on earth.

OCTOBER 6
Our Actions Follow Our Faith

LET us do our duty as it presents itself. This is the secret of true faith and peace. Suppose a religious man, for instance, is in the society of strangers. He takes things as they come, discourses naturally, and does good according to each opportunity. His heart is in his work and his thoughts rest without effort on his God and Savior. This is the way of a Christian.

—*Saving Knowledge*

PRAYER. Enliven my faith, O Lord, so that my heart may ever be at peace, knowing that I am striving to do my duty to You and my neighbor.

OCTOBER 7
Christage Present in the Eucharist

WHAT is it that is vouchsafed to us at the Holy Table when we commemorate the Lord's death? It is "Jesus Christ before our eyes evidently set forth, crucified among us" (Gal 3:1).

We need no visible miracle to convince us of the Presence of the Lord Incarnate. We have faith and love enough to "discern the Lord's Body" (1 Cor 11:29). He Who is at the right hand of God manifests Himself as really and fully as if He were visibly there. —*State of Grace*

PRAYER. *Blessed Savior, never let me grow complacent in receiving You in Communion. May I always rejoice in this great privilege.*

OCTOBER 8
Grace Does Not Force

IN truth, the two doctrines of the sovereign and overruling power of divine grace and man's power of resistance need not at all interfere with each other. They lie in different provinces.

Thus St. Paul accounted them; else he could not have introduced a text with the exhortation, "Work out" or accomplish "your own salvation with fear and trembling, for it is God Who works" or acts "in you" (Phil 2:12). —*Human Responsibility*

PRAYER. *Your grace prompts me, O God, to shun evil and do good. May I ever freely cooperate with Your inspirations.*

OCTOBER 9
Effects of Serious Sin

CHRIST has healed each of us and has said to us, "See that you sin no more lest a worse thing come to you" (Jn 5:14). If we commit sin, we fall—not at once back into the unredeemed and lost world. No, but at least we fall out of the Kingdom.

We fall into what will lead us back into the lost world, unless we turn heavenward and extricate ourselves from our fearful state as speedily as we can. —*State of Salvation*

PRAYER. *Dear Lord, if I should have the misfortune of sinning seriously, let me seek Your forgiveness in the Sacrament of Reconciliation.*

OCTOBER 10
Danger of Worldly Possessions

THE most obvious danger which worldly possessions present to our spiritual welfare is that they become practically a substitute in our hearts for that One Object to which our supreme devotion is due. They are present; God is unseen.

Even Religious men cannot easily rid themselves of a secret feeling that wealth gives them an importance, a superiority; and in consequence they get attached to this world and lose sight of the duty of bearing the Cross. —*Danger of Riches*

PRAYER. *Christ, my Savior, I know that the things of this world have been given to us for the good of all. Help me to be generous in using them.*

OCTOBER 11
Daily Life Can Save

WHEN a man begins to feel he has a soul, and a work to do, and a reward to be gained, he says, "What must I *do* to please God?" And sometimes he is led to think he ought to be useful on a large scale, and goes out of his line of life, that he may be doing something worth doing, as he considers it.

We need not give up our usual manner of life in order to serve God. The most humble and quietest station is acceptable to Him. —*Guilelessness*

PRAYER. *Let me ever be conscious, O Lord, that the duties of my state in life can be a means of growing closer to You.*

OCTOBER 12
Watch and Pray

HOW many are there who bear half the trial God puts on them, but not the whole of it; who go on well for a time, and then fall away! Saul bore on for seven days, and fainted not; on the eighth day his faith failed him.

Oh, may we persevere to the end! Let us watch and pray. Let us not think it enough to have got through one temptation well; through our whole life we are on trial. —*Trial of Saul*

PRAYER. *Heavenly Father, keep me away from presumption. Let me watch and pray that I may persevere to the end.*

OCTOBER 13
God Loved Us First

BAPTISM placed you in this blessed state. God did not wait till you should do some good thing before He blessed you. No! He knew you could do no good thing of yourselves. So He came to you first; He loved you before you loved Him. He placed you in a new and heavenly state, in which, while you remain, you are safe.

He first gives, and then commands; He tells us to obey Him, not to gain His favor, but in order not to lose it. —*Call of David*

PRAYER. *God of love, help me to imitate Your merciful love for us by a selfless love for my neighbor.*

OCTOBER 14
Striving for Holiness

THIS is the object which is set before us, to become holy as He Who has called us is holy, and to discipline and chasten ourselves in order that we may become so.

We may be quite sure, that unless we chasten ourselves, God will chasten us. If we judge ourselves, through His mercy we shall not be judged by Him. If we do not set about changing ourselves by gentle measures, He will change us by severe remedies. —*Yoke of Christ*

PRAYER. *Blessed Lord, let every day be spent in a genuine attempt to remove from my life anything that separates me from You.*

OCTOBER 15
Receiving the Sacraments

WHEN we feel reluctant to serve God, when thoughts rise within us as if He were a hard Master, let us recollect that we, as being Christians, are not in the flesh, but in the Spirit, and let us act upon the conviction of it.

Let us come to the ordinances of grace, in which Christ gives His Holy Spirit, to enable us to do that which by nature we cannot do, and to be "the servants of righteousness."

—*Strictness of Law of Christ*

PRAYER. *Dear Jesus, You have instituted the Sacraments as a means of imparting Your grace. Let me always receive them devoutly.*

OCTOBER 16
Sin Leads to Unbelief

A MAN who loves sin does not wish the Gospel to be true, and therefore is not a fair judge of it.

A mere man of the world, a selfish and covetous man, or a drunkard, or an extortioner, is, from a sense of interest, against that Bible which condemns him, and would account that man indeed a messenger of good tidings of peace who could prove to him that Christ's doctrine was not from God.

—*Inward Witness*

PRAYER. *Triune God, the Bible is Your love letter to the world. Draw all sinners close to You that they may feel Your mercy and believe in You.*

OCTOBER 17
Patience in Trials

E have not learned the duty of waiting and being still. Great perils, just now, encompass the Church; what ought we to do? Doubtless to meet them with all the wisdom and prudence in our power. But, after all, is not our main duty to go on quietly and steadfastly in our old ways, as if nothing was the matter?

Let our resolve be, if we are to perish, it shall be at our post of duty. —*Willfulness of Israel*

PRAYER. *O God, I am impatient so often with what is happening in Your Church. Let me not be disturbed but possess my soul in patience.*

OCTOBER 18
Truth and Power in Scripture

HE Bible, then, seems to say—God is not a hard master to require belief, without affording grounds for believing; only follow your own sense of right, and you will gain from that very obedience a conviction of the truth and power of that Redeemer Whom a supernatural message has revealed.

You will most assuredly be led on into all the truth: you will recognize the force, meaning, and awful graciousness of the Gospel Creed.

—*Inward Witness*

PRAYER. *Lord Jesus, You are the Word of God. When I read the Scriptures, let me see You on every page and learn to become more like You.*

OCTOBER 19
A Little Learning Is Dangerous

A LITTLE learning is a dangerous thing. When men think they know more than others, they often talk for the sake of talking, and they speak lightly of the All-Holy God, to gratify their self-conceit and vanity.

And often it answers no purpose to dispute with such persons, for they will assent to nothing you can say. They have no common ground with you, and when they talk of religion they are like blind persons talking of colors. —*Inward Witness*

PRAYER. *Humble Savior, keep me from pride and vanity of all kinds. May I never be puffed up by learning and knowledge.*

OCTOBER 20
Act on Gospel Truths

HOW dangerous their state is who are content to take the truths of the Gospel on trust, without caring whether or not those truths are realized in their own heart and conduct.

Such men, when assailed by ridicule and sophistry, are likely to fall; they have no root in themselves; and should they fall away from the faith, it will be a slight thing at the last day to plead that they were altogether unprepared and ignorant. —*Inward Witness*

PRAYER. *Almighty God, You want us to be doers of Your Word and not hearers only. Give me strength to always do Your will.*

OCTOBER 21
We Sow, Others Reap

T O expect great effects from our exertions for religious objects is natural indeed, and innocent, but it arises from inexperience of the kind of work we have to do—to change the heart and will of man.

It is a far nobler frame of mind to labor, not with the hope of seeing the fruit of our labor, but for conscience' sake, as a matter of duty; and again, in faith, trusting good will be done, though we see it not. The time for reaping what we have sown is hereafter, not here. *—Jeremiah a Lesson*

PRAYER. O Jesus, let me labor in Your vineyard to make You known and loved more. I may not see fruit, but You will bring it forth in due season.

OCTOBER 22
Gain after Pain

A ND as in sickness sharp remedies are often used, so it is with our souls; we must go through pain, we must practice self-denial, we must curb our wills and purify our hearts, before we are capable of any lasting solid peace.

To attempt to gain happiness, except in this way, is a labor lost; it is building on the sand; the foundation will soon give way, though the house looks fair for a time. *—Jeremiah a Lesson*

PRAYER. Compassionate Father, teach me to regard all suffering as something allowed by You to make me more like Your Son Jesus.

OCTOBER 23
Giving Good Example

GIVE not over your attempts to serve God, though you see nothing come of them. Watch and pray, and obey your conscience, though you cannot perceive your own progress in holiness. Go on, and you cannot but go forward.

Let your light shine before men, and praise God by a consistent life, even though others do not seem to glorify their Father on account of it, or to be benefited by your example. —*Jeremiah a Lesson*

PRAYER. *Father, You will that all people should be saved. Help me to be zealous for the salvation of all by my life-witness and by my prayer.*

OCTOBER 24
Value of Earthly Life

WHEN persons are convinced that life is short, that it is unequal to any great purpose, when they feel that the next life is all in all, then they are apt to undervalue this life altogether, and to forget its real importance.

Yet it should be recollected that the employments of this world, though not themselves heavenly, are, after all, the way to heaven—though not the fruit, are the seed of immortality!

—*Doing Glory to God*

PRAYER. *O Lord, let me make the most of every moment given me. May I build up eternity with the moments You allot to me on earth.*

OCTOBER 25
Meditation Should Lead to Action

IT is difficult steadily to contemplate the life to come, yet to act in this. Those who meditate are likely to neglect those active duties which are, in fact, incumbent on them, and to dwell upon the thought of God's glory, till they forget to act to His glory.

This state of mind is chided in the words of the holy Angels to the Apostles, when they say, "You men of Galilee, why stand you gazing up into heaven?" (Acts 1:11).   —*Doing Glory to God*

PRAYER. *Self-revealing God, let me rely always on Your all-enlightening Word. Help me to ponder it well and put it into practice in my daily life.*

OCTOBER 26
Misguided Spirituality

A MAN may come to fancy that to lose taste and patience for the businesses of this life is renouncing the world and becoming spiritually minded. And he fancies that it is absolutely necessary to renounce all earnestness or activity in his worldly employments.

Altogether he looks upon his worldly occupation simply as a burden and a cross, and the sooner he can release himself from it, so much the better.   —*Doing Glory to God*

PRAYER. *Dear Jesus, Your Apostle Paul said: "Whatever you do, in word or deed, do it for the Lord" (Col 3:17). Help me to follow his counsel.*

OCTOBER 27
Let Christ Be Your Glory

GO on, then, contentedly in the path of duty, seeking Christ in His house and in His ordinances, and He will be your glory at His coming. He will own you before His Father.

Let the world record the names of heroes, and reward courage, and ability, and skill, and perseverance, with its proud titles of honor. Verily, these have their reward. Your names will be written in heaven. —*Vanity of Human Glory*

PRAYER. *Lord of glory, help me to attain the crown of glory You hold out to me by seeking You above all things.*

OCTOBER 28
Seeking True Wisdom

WHAT religious opinion can be named which some men or other have not at some time held? All are equally confident in the truth of their own doctrines.

Let not the diversity of opinion in the world dismay you, or deter you from seeking all your life long true wisdom. It is not a search for this day or that, but as you should ever grow in grace, so should you ever grow also in the knowledge of our Lord and Savior Jesus Christ. —*Truth Hidden*

PRAYER. *Father of every good gift, send Your Spirit upon me that I may grow in the knowledge of Jesus, Your Son, and love Him more.*

OCTOBER 29
Time of Rest Is Hereafter

ET us be willing to endure toil and trouble; and should times of comparative quiet be given to us, or the Spirit of comfort poured upon us, let us not inconsiderately rest in these accidental blessings.

While we thank God for them, let us remember that in its turn the time of labor and fear, and danger and anxiety, will come upon us. The time of eternal rest will come hereafter. —*Truth Hidden*

PRAYER. *Loving Father, grant me a true fervor in Your service. Let me never tire of following Your Son's example and avoiding evil.*

OCTOBER 30
Conscience and the Gospel

HRIST replied, "You are not far from the Kingdom of God" (Mk 12:34), i.e., you are not far from being a Christian.

In these words, then, we are taught, first, that the Christian's faith and obedience are not the same religion as that of natural conscience, as being some way beyond it; secondly, that this way is "not far," not far in the case of those who try to act up to their conscience; in other words, that obedience to conscience leads to obedience to the Gospel. —*Obedience to God*

PRAYER. *O Lord, grant me the grace to follow Your Commandments of love. and justice found in the Gospel and so be worthy of the joys of heaven.*

OCTOBER 31
False Hopes

E see the hopelessness of waiting for any sudden change of heart, if we are at present living in sin. Far more persons thus deceive themselves than at first sight may appear.

There are even many irreligious men who look forward for a possible day when God will change their hearts by His own mere power, in spite of themselves, and who thus get rid of the troublesome thought that now they are in a state of fearful peril. —*Obedience to God*

PRAYER. *Dear God, bless me with true hope that I may act as if everything depended upon me and pray as if everything depended on You.*

NOVEMBER 1
Joining the Saints in Glory

HE day will come at length, when our Lord and Savior will unveil that Sacred Countenance to the whole world, which no sinner ever yet could see and live. Then will the world be forced to look upon Him, Whom they pierced.

We shall see our Lord, and His Blessed Mother, the Apostles and Prophets, and all those righteous men whom we now read of in history, and long to know. —*Reverence Due to Mary*

PRAYER. *Let me, O Lord, one day, look upon the face of my Savior and His Blessed Mother, in heaven. Make me worthy of His promises.*

159

NOVEMBER 2
Waiting for Jesus at Death

THOUGH Jesus delays His coming, let us watch for Him in the cold and dreariness which must one day have an end. Attend His summons we must, at any rate, when He strips us of the body. Let us anticipate, by a voluntary act, what will one day come on us of necessity.

Let us wait for Him solemnly, hopefully, patiently, obediently. Let us be resigned to His will, while active in good works. —*Worship*

PRAYER. *Every day of my life, dear Savior, should be one of anticipation for Your coming again. Let me always be prepared.*

NOVEMBER 3
Seek Him Where He May Be Found

R again, we fancy that the means of gaining heaven are something stranger and rarer than the mere obvious duty of obedience to God.

We are loath to seek Christ in the waters of Jordan rather than in Pharpar and Abana, rivers of Damascus; we prefer to seek Him in the height above, or to descend into the deep, rather than to believe that the Word is nigh us, even in our mouth and in our heart. —*Obedience to God*

PRAYER. *Dear Jesus, You have told us that we will find You when we seek You with all our heart. Grant that I may seek You, find You, and never be separated from You.*

NOVEMBER 4
The Face of Christ

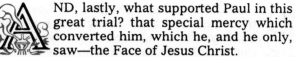

ND, lastly, what supported Paul in this great trial? that special mercy which converted him, which he, and he only, saw—the Face of Jesus Christ.

That all-pitying, all-holy eye, which turned in love upon St. Peter when he denied Him, and thereby roused him to repentance, looked on St. Paul also, while he persecuted Him, and wrought in him a sudden conversion. "Last of all," he says, "He was seen by me also, as by one born out of due time" (1 Cor 15:8).

—Sudden Conversions

PRAYER. *According to Scripture, dear Jesus, St. Paul was privileged to see Your holy face after Your Ascension. Grant that I may see You face to face someday in heaven.*

NOVEMBER 5
Watchful Ears and a Willing Heart

HRIST is our Shepherd, and the sheep know His voice. If we are His sheep, we shall hear it, recognize it, and obey it.

Let us beware of not following when He goes before. Let us beware of receiving His grace in vain. Let us us desire to know His voice; let us pray for the gift of watchful ears and a willing heart. *—Shepherd of Our Souls*

PRAYER. *Grant that I may always follow You as my Shepherd, dear Jesus. Let me hear Your voice with watchful ears and a willing heart.*

NOVEMBER 6
Blessed Are They Who Turn to God

BLESSED are they who give the flower of their days and their strength of soul and body to Christ; blessed are they who in their youth turn to Him Who gave His life for them, and would fain give it to them and implant it in them, that they may live forever.

Blessed are they who resolve—come good, come evil, come sunshine, come tempest, come honor, come dishonor—that He shall be their Lord and Master, their King and God!

—Shepherd of Our Souls

PRAYER. *Beloved Savior, Who suffered and died for me, You are my all in all. Teach me how to give myself, to abandon myself to You.*

NOVEMBER 7
Being Content with What We Are

IT is plain that the temptation under which man fell in paradise was this, an ambitious curiosity after knowledge which was not allowed him. Man sought to share in what God was, but he could not without ceasing to be what God was also—holy and perfect.

But man shared in God's knowledge by losing His image. Our happiness as well as duty lies in being contented with what we are—with what God makes us. *—Ignorance of Evil*

PRAYER. *All-merciful God, I want to be content with what I am, with what You will make me. Therefore I abandon myself to You.*

NOVEMBER 8
Worship and Service

WE know that Angels cry Holy, Holy, Holy and that they do God's bidding. Worship and service make up their blessedness, and such is our blessedness in proportion as we approach them.

But all exercises of mind which lead us to reflect upon what worship is, and why we worship; what service is, and why we serve, tend to divert our minds from the one thing needful. Truly religious minds turn inquiry into meditation, exhortation into worship, and argument into teaching. —*Ignorance of Evil*

PRAYER. Loving Father, at Mass "we join with all the choirs of heaven as they sing forever to Your glory." May I always be grateful for this privilege.

NOVEMBER 9
Obeying God's Call

THIS, then, is the lesson taught us by St. Paul's conversion, promptly to obey the call. If we do obey it, to God be the glory, for He it is Who works in us. If we do not obey, to ourselves be all the shame, for sin and unbelief work in us.

Let us take care to act accordingly—being exceedingly alarmed lest we should *not* obey God's voice when He calls us, yet not taking credit to ourselves if we *do* obey it. —*Divine Calls*

PRAYER. Merciful God, by Your grace help me to imitate St. Paul and promptly obey Your calls.

NOVEMBER 10
Knowledge Leads to Action

E may be in the practice of reading Scripture carefully and trying to serve God, and its sense may, as if suddenly, break upon us, in a way it never did before.

We may be able to enter into the manner of life of the early Christians and to understand that it is very different from the life which men live now. Now knowledge is a call to action; an insight into the way of perfection is a call to perfection. —*Divine Calls*

PRAYER. *Lord, grant me light to know Your will and grace to do and love Your will each day.*

NOVEMBER 11
The Armor of God

UR weapons are simple and powerful. The Lord's Prayer is one such weapon when we are tempted to sin. One or two holy texts, such as our Savior used when He was tempted by the devil, is another.

The Sacrament of the Lord's Supper is another such, and greater; holy, mysterious, life-giving, but equally simple. What is so simple as a little bread and a little wine? But, in the hands of the Spirit of God, it is the power of God unto salvation. —*Call of David*

PRAYER. *God of goodness, grant that I will never fail to use the powerful weapons You have put at our disposal to resist evil.*

NOVEMBER 12
First Thoughts May Be Best

NOW our great security against sin lies in being shocked at it. It is sometimes said, "Second thoughts are best." This is true in many cases; but there are times when it is very false, and when, on the contrary, first thoughts are best.

At first, our conscience tells us, in a plain straightforward way, what is right and what is wrong. But when we trifle with this warning, our reason becomes perverted and deceives us to our ruin. —*Curiosity a Temptation*

PRAYER. *Holy Spirit, Spirit of Light and Love, Spirit of Truth, help me to form a right conscience and to follow it promptly when danger is near.*

NOVEMBER 13
Hardened Hearts

THIS is our state; and perhaps so it is that, as the Israelites for forty years hardened their hearts in the wilderness, in spite of the manna and the quails, so we for years have been hardening ours in spite of the spiritual gifts which are the portion of Christians.

Instead of listening to the voice of conscience, instead of availing ourselves of the aid of heavenly grace, we have gone on year after year with the vain dream of turning to God some future day. —*Miracles No Remedy*

PRAYER. *Oh that today I will hear Your voice, O Lord, and harden not my heart!*

NOVEMBER 14
Truth of the Bible

WE may sometimes hear men say, "How do you know that the Bible is true? You are told so in church; your parents believed it; but might they not be mistaken? and if so, you are mistaken also."

Now to this objection it may be answered, and very satisfactorily, "Is it then nothing toward convincing us of the truth of the Gospel, that those whom we love best and reverence most believe it?"
—Inward Witness

PRAYER. *O Holy Spirit, Spirit of Truth, may I ever be inspired by the truths of Sacred Scripture.*

NOVEMBER 15
Knowledge through Obedience

THE Psalmist declares that in consequence of having obeyed God's Commandments he had obtained more understanding than those who had first enlightened his ignorance.

As if he said, "When I was a child, they were careful that I should not only know my duty, but do it. And this obedience to His Commandments has brought me to a clearer knowledge of His truth than any mere instruction could convey."
—Inward Witness

PRAYER. *Heavenly Father, grant that I may believe what I have learned and practice what I believe and so come to know and love You more.*

NOVEMBER 16
Sorrowful Yet Rejoicing

OW, I know full well that this whole subject is distasteful to many men, who say we ought to be cheerful. "We are bid rejoice, why then do you bid us mourn?"

I bid you mourn in order that you may rejoice more perfectly. Take up the Cross of Christ, that you may wear His crown. Give your hearts to Him, and you will see how Christians can be sorrowful, yet always rejoicing. —*Jeremiah a Lesson*

PRAYER. *Lord of glory, teach me how to rejoice amid sorrow while on earth. Let me always focus on the eternal bliss that I hope to share with You.*

NOVEMBER 17
Professing Christ to Others

AM quite sure that none of us, even the best, have resisted the world as we ought to have done. Our faces have not been like flints; we have been afraid of men's words, and dismayed at their looks, and we have yielded to them at times against our better judgment.

Let us beg God to teach us *how* to confess Him before men; lest if we deny Him now, He may deny us before the Angels of God hereafter. —*Endurance of Censure*

PRAYER. *Lord God of Hosts, may everything I do contribute to Your greater glory and bring others to You.*

NOVEMBER 18
We Can Do Nothing without God

RECOLLECT that you cannot do any one thing of all the duties I have been speaking of, without God's help. Anyone who attempts to resist the world, or to do other good things by his own strength, will be sure to fall.

We *can* do good things, but it is when God gives us power to do them. Therefore we must pray to Him for the power. When we are brought into temptation of any kind, we should lift up our hearts to God.   —*Endurance of Censure*

PRAYER. *Heavenly Father, let me call upon Your help before undertaking to do anything in my life. For without You I can do nothing.*

NOVEMBER 19
God Gives by Measure and Season

ACT up to your light, though in the midst of difficulties, and you will be carried on, you do not know how far.

Abraham obeyed the call and journeyed, not knowing whither he went; so we, if we follow the voice of God, shall be brought on step by step into a new world, of which before we had no idea. This is His gracious way with us; He gives, not all at once, but by measure and season, wisely.   —*Truth Hidden*

PRAYER. *Lord Jesus, grant me a strong faith and an unwavering trust in You. Help me especially when all is in darkness and You seem far away.*

NOVEMBER 20
Preferring Eternity to the Present

WHEN Christ comes at last, blessed indeed will be the lot of him who has joined himself to Him. He has risked the present against the future, preferring the chance of eternity to the certainty of time. Then his reward will be but beginning when that of the children of this world is come to an end.

In the words of the wise man, "Then shall the righteous man be numbered among the children of God, and his lot be among the Saints!" (Wis 5:1-5). —*Moral Effects of Communion*

PRAYER. *Help me, O Lord, to realize that this life, with its passing pleasures, is no match for the life You have prepared for those who love You.*

NOVEMBER 21
Repent of Our Sins

IF we, through God's unspeakable gift, have in any measure followed Mary's innocence in our youth, let us bless Him Who enabled us. But so far as we are conscious of having departed from Him, let us bewail our guilt.

Let us acknowledge from the heart that no punishment is too severe for us, no chastisement should be unwelcome, if it tends to burn away the corruption within us. —*Reverence Due to Mary*

PRAYER. *Your Blessed Mother, O Jesus, was preserved free from all sin. By her prayers and example may I follow You more closely.*

NOVEMBER 22
Grow Where You Are Planted

I AM speaking of cases when it is a person's duty to remain in his worldly calling, and he does remain in it but cherishes dissatisfaction with it. What he ought to feel is this— that *while* in it he is to glorify God, not *out* of it, but *in* it, and by *means* of it.

The Lord Jesus is best served when men are not slothful in business, but do their duty in that state of life in which it has pleased God to call them. —*Doing Glory to God*

PRAYER. Lord Jesus, guard me from the desire to take the easy way. Let me follow You in the way and in the place that You have chosen.

NOVEMBER 23
Attitude in Church

WHEN Moses came down from Mount Sinai, where he had been forty days and forty nights, his face quite shone and dazzled the people, so that he was obliged to put a veil over it.

Such is the effect of God's grace on those who come to church in faith and love; their mode of acting and talking, their very manner and behavior, show they have been in God's presence. They are ever sober, cheerful, modest, serious, and earnest. —*Reverence in Worship*

PRAYER. I am often in Your Eucharistic presence, dear Jesus. By Your grace let Your light shine forth in me.

NOVEMBER 24
Christ Calls Many Times

FOR in truth we are not called once only, but many times; all through our life Christ is calling us. He called us first in Baptism; but afterward also, whether we obey His voice or not, He calls us still.

If we fall from our Baptism, He calls us to repent; if we are striving to fulfill our calling, He calls us on from grace to grace, and from holiness to holiness, while life is given us.—*Divine Calls*

PRAYER. *Dear Savior, I am truly grateful for the ways in which You call us and watch over us. Let me show my love by being faithful to You.*

NOVEMBER 25
Conscientiousness

NOW what is this strict virtue called? It is called *faith*. It is no matter whether we call it faith or conscientiousness, they are in substance one and the same. Where there is faith, there is conscientiousness. They may be distinguished from each other in words, but they are not divided in fact.

They belong to one habit of mind—dutifulness; they show themselves in obedience, in the careful, anxious observance of God's will, however we learn it. —*Josiah a Pattern*

PRAYER. *O my Lord, let me see Your will as all love no matter where it leads. Deepen my faith that I may always do and love Your will.*

NOVEMBER 26
Divine Providence

IF we could see the course of God's dispensations in this world, as the Angels see them, we should not be able to deny that it was His unseen hand that ordered them.

This is what moves the Saints in the Apocalypse to praise and adore Almighty God—the view of His wonderful works seen as a whole from first to last. "Great and marvellous are Your works, Lord God Almighty; just and true are Your ways" (Rv 15:3-4). —*Kingdom of the Saints*

PRAYER. *Dear Jesus, let me one day praise You with Your Holy Mother and all the Saints in Your heavenly Kingdom.*

NOVEMBER 27
No Looking Back

WE are by nature weakened and helpless. We cannot please God; we cannot move hand or foot. He says not to us, "Get well first, and I will receive you," but He begins a cure in us and receives us.

Then He says, "Take care not to go back; take care of yourselves; beware of a relapse; keep out of danger." Such then is your state, my brethren, unless you have fallen from Christ.

—*Call of David*

PRAYER. *God of holiness, pour down upon me the graces I need to follow Your Son Jesus. Let me follow Him and never look back.*

NOVEMBER 28
The Gift of Baptism

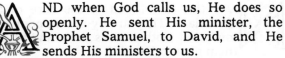

AND when God calls us, He does so openly. He sent His minister, the Prophet Samuel, to David, and He sends His ministers to us.

He sends His ministers to those whom He has from eternity chosen. He does not say to them, "Fill your horn with oil" (1 Sm 16:1), but "Fill your font with water." For as He chose David by pouring oil upon his head, so does He choose us by Baptism. —*Call of David*

PRAYER. *How can I thank You, Merciful God, for the precious gift of Baptism! I will try to show my gratitude by being faithful to my baptismal promises.*

NOVEMBER 29
The Final Judgment

THIS we know to be our own fearful lot, that before us lies a time when we must see our Maker and Lord face to face. We are destined to come before Him in judgment, and that on our first meeting.

We are not merely to be rewarded or punished, we are to be judged. We have to stand before His righteous Presence, and that one by one. One by one we shall have to endure His holy and searching eye. —*Worship*

PRAYER. *Be merciful to me, Blessed Savior, when I meet You in judgment. Let not my sins be cause for separating myself from You.*

NOVEMBER 30
Mystery of God's Election

NOW this is fulfilled in the case of all Christians. They are by nature poor and lowly but God chooses them and brings them near to Himself.

Why He chooses these men and passes over those, we know not. Some men are born within the bounds of holy Church, and are baptized with her Baptism; others are not even baptized at all. God has chosen all of us to salvation, not for our righteousness, but for His great mercies.

— *Call of David*

PRAYER. *Your ways are not our ways, Almighty God. Though I understand not, let me always praise Your mercy.*

DECEMBER 1
Divine Calls

DIVINE calls in Scripture require instant obedience, and next call us we know not to what; call us on in the darkness. Faith alone can obey them.

How does this concern us now? We were all called to serve God in infancy, before we could obey or disobey; we have been called to a state of salvation, through Holy Baptism, by the act of our parents. Calling is not a thing future with us, but a thing past. —*Divine Calls*

PRAYER. *Sometimes I am afraid, dear Lord, when You lead me on in darkness. Increase my little faith that I may ever trust in You.*

174

DECEMBER 2
Sacraments—Invisible Miracles

CHRISTIANS too have miracles, but they are not outward but inward. Ours are not miracles of evidence, but of power and influence. Ours are invisible, and are exercised upon the soul. They consist in the Sacraments, and they just do that very thing which the Jewish miracles did not.

The supernatural works which God does toward us are in the heart, and impart grace; and if we disobey, we are not disobeying His command only, but resisting His presence.

—Miracles No Remedy

PRAYER. *Merciful God, let me make frequent use of the wonderful Sacraments of Penance and Holy Communion and thus grow in Your grace.*

DECEMBER 3
Temples of the Spirit

WHEN Christ's ministers baptize, the Spirit of the Lord comes upon the child baptized henceforth; nay, dwells in him, for the Christian's gift is far greater even than David's.

God's Spirit did but come upon David, and visit him from time to time; but He vouchsafes to dwell within the Christian, so as to make his heart and body His temple. *—Call of David*

PRAYER. *Lord Jesus, make me a vessel of honor after the example of Your Holy Mother, so that Your Holy Spirit will dwell in me.*

DECEMBER 4
Resist at the Beginning

WHEN I say resist the beginnings of evil, I do not mean the first act merely, but the rising thought of evil. Whatever the temptation may be, there may be no time to wait and gaze without being caught.

Directly we are made aware of the temptation, we shall, if we are wise, turn our backs upon it without waiting to think and reason about it. We shall engage our mind in other thoughts. —*Curiosity a Temptation*

PRAYER. *Dear Jesus, You taught us to ask the Father to "deliver us from evil." Strengthen me in temptation for I can do nothing without You.*

DECEMBER 5
Christians—Heirs of Promise

CHRISTIANS are elected out of the world, in Jesus Christ our Savior, to a glory incomprehensible and eternal. We are the heirs of promise; God has loved us before we were born.

He had us taken into His Church in our infancy. He by Baptism made us new creatures, giving us powers which we by nature had not and raising us to the unseen society of Saints and Angels. —*Josiah a Pattern*

PRAYER. *O Lord, let my soul praise You that it may love You. Let it recount to You Your mercies that it may praise You for them all.*

DECEMBER 6
Value of Good Example

THOSE who do not serve God with a single heart know they ought to do so, and they do not like to be reminded that they ought.

And when they fall in with anyone who does live to God, he serves to remind them of it, and that is unpleasant to them, and that is the first reason why they are angry with a religious man. The sight of him disturbs them and makes them uneasy.   —*Endurance of Censure*

PRAYER. Loving Father, help me to be encouraged by the good example of my brothers and sisters who serve You faithfully.

DECEMBER 7
Success through Failure

ALL the Prophets were not Teachers merely, but Confessors. They came not merely to unfold the Law, or to foretell the Gospel, but to warn and rebuke; nor to rebuke only, but to suffer.

This world is a scene of conflict between good and evil. The evil not only avoids but persecutes the good; the good cannot conquer except by suffering. Good men seem to fail; their cause triumphs, but their own overthrow is the price paid for this success.   —*Endurance of Censure*

PRAYER. Dear Jesus, teach my heart that peace comes not by running away from the Cross but by embracing it.

DECEMBER 8
The Immaculate Conception

IT is difficult for me to comprehend a person who *understands* the doctrine of the Immaculate Conception and yet objects to it. Does not the objector consider that *Eve* was created *without* original sin? Does he not believe that St. John Baptist had the grace of God even before his birth? What do we believe of Mary, but that grace was given her from the first moment of her existence?

We do not say that she did not owe her salvation to the death of her Son. We say that she is the fruit of His Passion. —*Memorandum*

PRAYER. *Dear Jesus, help me to imitate Your Immaculate Virgin Mother in her love for You.*

DECEMBER 9
God Speaks to Us

GOD, and none other but He, speaks first in our consciences, then in His Holy Word. And lest we should be in any difficulty about the matter, He has most mercifully told us so in Scripture.

He refers to the great Moral Law as the foundation of the truth, which His Apostles and Prophets, and last of all His Son, have taught us: "Fear God, and keep His Commandments; for this is the whole duty of man."

—*Obedience to God*

PRAYER. *Heavenly Father, inspire me to meditate on Your holy words every day.*

DECEMBER 10
Son of Man

NO earthly images can come up to the awful and gracious truth that God became the Son of Man—that the Word became flesh and was born of a woman.

No titles of earth can Christ give to Himself, ever so lowly or mean, which will fitly show us His condescension. Yet He delights in conveying to us some notion of the degradation, hardship, and pain, which He underwent for our sake. —*Shepherd of Our Souls*

PRAYER. *Invisible God, help me to see Jesus made flesh as a visible reflection of You.*

DECEMBER 11
Christ—Lowly, Wise, and Brave

CHRIST, too, not only suffered with Jacob, and was in contemplation with Moses, but fought and conquered with David. David defended his father's sheep at Bethlehem; Christ, born and heralded to the shepherds at Bethlehem, suffered on the Cross in order to conquer.

Jacob was not as David, nor David as Jacob, nor either of them as Moses; but Christ was all three, as fulfilling all types, the lowly Jacob, the wise Moses, the heroic David, all in one—Priest, Prophet, and King. —*Shepherd of Our Souls*

PRAYER. *Loving Savior, deliver me from pride, bless me with true wisdom, and give me a courageous heart to follow You.*

DECEMBER 12
No More Searching

IF we consult the historians, philosophers, and poets of this world, we shall be led to think great men happy. We shall consider that the highest course of life is the mere pursuit, not the enjoyment of good.

We have not to seek our highest good. It is found! It is brought near us in the descent of the Son of God from His Father's bosom to this world. —*Religious Joy*

PRAYER. Heavenly Father, in contemplating the birth of Your Son in time and in the Eucharist, may I ever attain a new spiritual birth.

DECEMBER 13
Using This World Wisely

TO the true Christian the world assumes an interesting appearance. It is a scene of probation. Every soul is a candidate for immortality.

The more we realize this view of things, the more we shall be led habitually to pray that upon every Christian may descend not merely worldly goods but that heavenly grace which alone can turn this world to good account for us and make it the path of peace and of life everlasting. —*Temporal Advantages*

PRAYER. I know that I have an eternal destiny with You, O God. Let my actions be a cause of my merit and an influence on others for their eternal salvation.

DECEMBER 14
The Law of Christ

A CHRISTIAN goes by a law which others know not; not his own wisdom or judgment but Christ's wisdom and the judgment of the Spirit. It is imparted to him by that inward perception of truth and duty which is the rule of his reason, affections, wishes, tastes, and all that is in him, and which is the result of persevering obedience.

This it is which gives so unearthly a character to his whole life and conversation.

—*Subjection of Reason*

PRAYER. *O Lord, let me be open to the promptings of Your grace. May I always know Your will and have the courage to carry it out.*

DECEMBER 15
An Honest and Good Heart

PRAY to Jesus to give you what Scripture calls "an honest and good heart," and, without waiting, begin at once to obey Him with the best heart you have.

Obedience is the only way of seeking Him. All your duties are obediences. If you are to believe the truths He has revealed, to regulate yourselves by His precepts, to adhere to His Church and people, why is it, except because *He* has bid you? —*Watching*

PRAYER. *Dear Jesus, I find it difficult always to obey Your laws and precepts. Assist me by Your grace to live up to Your expectations.*

DECEMBER 16
The Elect of God

A CERTAIN number of souls in the world, known to God, will obey the Truth when offered to them while others do not. These are God's special care [his elect].

They are the true Church, ever increasing in number as time goes on. With them lies the Communion of Saints. They have power with God. They are His armies who follow the Lamb, who overcome princes of the earth and who shall hereafter judge Angels. —*Visible Church*

PRAYER. *Dear Jesus, help me always to do Your bidding, so that I may be among those who find themselves at Your right hand at the Last Day.*

DECEMBER 17
Conforming Our Wills to God's

TAKING religion to mean being bound by God's law, the acting under God's will instead of our own—how few are there who even profess religion in this sense!

How few there are who live by any other rule than that of their own inclination and of external circumstances. With how few is the will of God an habitual object of thought, or search, or love, or obedience! —*Visible Church*

PRAYER. *O Lord, do not let me be influenced by the bad example of others. Grant that I may always be attentive to my religious duties.*

DECEMBER 18
Instruments of God

GOD'S instruments are poor and despised. The world hardly knows their names or not at all.

But there is an unseen connection in the Kingdom of God. They rise by falling. Plainly so, for no condescension *can* be so great as that of our Lord *Himself*. The more they abase themselves the more *like* they are to Him. The more like they are to Him, the greater must be their power with Him. —*Weapons of Saints*

PRAYER. Dear God, You choose the weak things of the world to do great things for Your Kingdom. Help me to be Your instrument.

DECEMBER 19
Waiting for Christ

IT must not be supposed, then, that the duty of waiting for our Lord's coming implies a neglect of our duties in this world. As it is possible to watch for Christ in spite of earthly reasonings to the contrary, so is it possible to engage in earthly duties, in spite of our watching.

Let us pray God to rule our hearts in this respect; that when He shall appear, we may have confidence, and not be ashamed before Him at His coming. —*Subjection of Reason*

PRAYER. Never let me deny You, O Lord, by my conduct before my friends so that You will not deny me when You come as my Judge.

DECEMBER 20
Delaying Repentance

MANY more than I have as yet mentioned wait for a time of repentance to come while at present they live in sin.

For instance the young, who consider it will be time enough to think of God when they grow old. Or those who confess they do not give that attention to religion which they ought to give. All such persons think that they will be able to seek Christ when they please!—*Obedience to God*

PRAYER. *God of mercy, teach me to make a daily examination of conscience. May I never delay asking Your forgiveness.*

DECEMBER 21
The Gospel and Us

THE Gospel leaves us just where it found us, as regards the necessity of our obedience to God; that Christ has not obeyed instead of us, but that obedience is quite as imperative as if Christ had never come.

Obedience is pressed upon us with additional sanctions; the difference being, not that He relaxes the strict rule of keeping His Commandments, but that He gives us spiritual aids, to enable us to keep them. —*Obedience to God*

PRAYER. *Lord Jesus, grant me Your grace to believe in the Gospel and to read it daily. Then let me put it into practice in my life.*

DECEMBER 22
Awaiting Our Infant Redeemer

ET us at this season approach Christ with awe and love, in Whom resides all perfection. Let us come to the Sanctifier to be sanctified.

At other seasons of the year we are reminded of watching, toiling, struggling, and suffering. But at this season we are reminded simply of God's gifts toward us sinners. This is a time for innocence, purity, gentleness, mildness, contentment, and peace. —*Mystery of Godliness*

PRAYER. *O God, in Your love for us, You promised to send a Redeemer. Now we await the Savior. Make me worthy to receive Him.*

DECEMBER 23
The Glory of Christmas

HRISTMAS is a time in which the whole Church seems decked in white, in her baptismal robe. Christ comes at other times with garments dyed in Blood. But now He comes to us in all serenity and peace, and He bids us to rejoice in Him and to love one another.

May each Christmas find us more and more like Him, Who at this time became a little Child for our sake, more humble, more holy, more happy, more full of God. —*Mystery of Godliness*

PRAYER. *Dear Jesus, by Your coming into the world as a Child, You have given us an example of living simply. Help me to imitate You.*

185

DECEMBER 24
Christ's Birth in Time

MAY it be our blessedness, as years go on, to add one grace to another and advance upward, step by step. The first grace is faith, the last is love.

First comes zeal, afterward comes loving-kindness. First comes humiliation, then comes peace. May we learn to mature all graces in us, watching and repenting because Christ is coming; joyful, thankful, and careless of the future because He is come.

—*Equanimity*

PRAYER. *Blessed Savior, Your coming into the world brought reconciliation to the human race. Let me enjoy the consolation of Your Presence in the world.*

DECEMBER 25
A Day of Great Joy

TAKE these thoughts with you, my brethren, to your homes on this festive day. It is a day of joy: it is good to be joyful—it is wrong to be otherwise.

For one day we may put off the burden of our polluted consciences, and rejoice in the perfections of our Savior Christ, without thinking of ourselves; but contemplating His glory, His righteousness, His purity, His majesty, His overflowing love. —*Religious Joy*

PRAYER. *Most loving Jesus, may I find all my joy in knowing, loving, and serving You.*

DECEMBER 26
Joy of the Shepherds

THE Angel honored a humble lot by his very appearing to the shepherds; next he taught it to be joyful. He disclosed good tidings so much above this world as to equalize high and low, rich and poor. He said, "Fear not."

The glory of God at first alarmed the shepherds, so he added the tidings of good, to work in them a more wholesome and happy temper. Then they rejoiced. —*Religious Joy*

PRAYER. Loving Father, may I also "fear not." Let me rejoice as I welcome Your Son.

DECEMBER 27
Poor Chosen as Heirs

CERTAIN shepherds were keeping watch over their flock by night, and Angels appeared to them. Why should the heavenly hosts appear to these shepherds? Were these shepherds learned, distinguished, or powerful? Nothing is said to make us think so.

The Angel appeared to teach them not to be downcast because they were low in the world. He appeared as if to show them that God had chosen the poor in this world to be heirs of His Kingdom. —*Religious Joy*

PRAYER. Heavenly Father, in celebrating the birth of Your Son, I rejoice that You have chosen the poor to be heirs of Your Kingdom.

DECEMBER 28
Smoothing Over Evil

WHAT is the very function of society, as it is at present, but a rude attempt to cover the degradation of the fall and to make men feel respect for themselves without returning to God.

I mean, not a sweeping away and cleansing out of corruption but a smoothing it over. Men give good names to what is evil, they indulge error, and bribe vice with the promise of bearing with it, so that it does but keep in the shade.

—Ignorance of Evil

PRAYER. *Merciful God, let me never smooth over my faults. Help me to acknowledge them, quickly repent, and return to You.*

DECEMBER 29
The Virtue of Simplicity

CHRIST has purchased for us what we lost in Adam, our garment of innocence. He has bid us and enabled us to become as little children; He has purchased for us the grace of *simplicity*.

We have a general idea what love is, and hope, and faith; but we are almost blind to what is one of the first elements of Christian perfection, that simple-mindedness which springs from the heart's being *whole* with God.—*Ignorance of Evil*

PRAYER. *Dear Jesus, may I have a childlike simplicity and always approach the Father as a loving child.*

DECEMBER 30
God's Mercy Endures Forever

LET us dwell upon times and seasons, times of trouble, times of joy, times of trial, times of refreshment. How did God cherish us as children!

How did He guide us in that dangerous time when the mind began to think for itself and the heart to open to the world! How did He with His sweet discipline restrain our passions and calm our fears! —*Remembrance of Past Mercies*

PRAYER. Blessed Savior, never let me neglect the grace You have given me over the course of my life. May I always be grateful for Your mercy.

DECEMBER 31
Our Happiness Depends on God

GOD knows what is my greatest happiness, but I do not. There is no rule about what is happy and good; what suits one would not suit another. And the ways by which perfection is reached vary very much; the medicines necessary for our souls are very different from each other.

Thus God leads us by strange ways; we know He wills our happiness, but we neither know what our happiness is, nor the way. We are blind; left to ourselves we would take the wrong way; we must leave it to Him. —*Meditations*

PRAYER. Almighty God, help me to know You, to love You, and to serve You in this world and to be happy with You forever in the next.

PRAYERS
Acts of Desire to Proclaim Christ

DEAR Jesus,
help me to spread Your fragrance everywhere I
go.
Flood my soul with Your Spirit and Life.
Penetrate and possess my whole being so utterly
that my life may only be a radiance of Yours.
Shine through me and be so in me
that every soul I come in contact with
may feel Your presence in my soul.

Let them look up,
and see no longer me,
but only Jesus!
Stay with me
and then I will begin to shine as You shine,
so to shine as to be a light to others.

The light,
O Jesus,
will be all from You;
none of it will be mine.
It will be You, shining on others through me.
Let me thus praise You
in the way which You love best,
by shining on those around me.
Let me preach You without preaching,
not by words but by example,
by the catching force,
the sympathetic influence of what I do,
the evident fullness of the love
my heart bears for You.